Keith Pepperell

Photographs V

Keith Pepperell

DEDICATION

As always to my spawn Jack, Lydia, and Alexandra

All of whom have snapped from time to time.

ACKNOWLEDGMENTS

Lady Joan Pepperell

Sir Francis Pepperell

Arthur MacDonald (Don) Fowler

Audrey Fowler

All of whom were a dab hand with a camera.

THE PHOTOGRAPHS

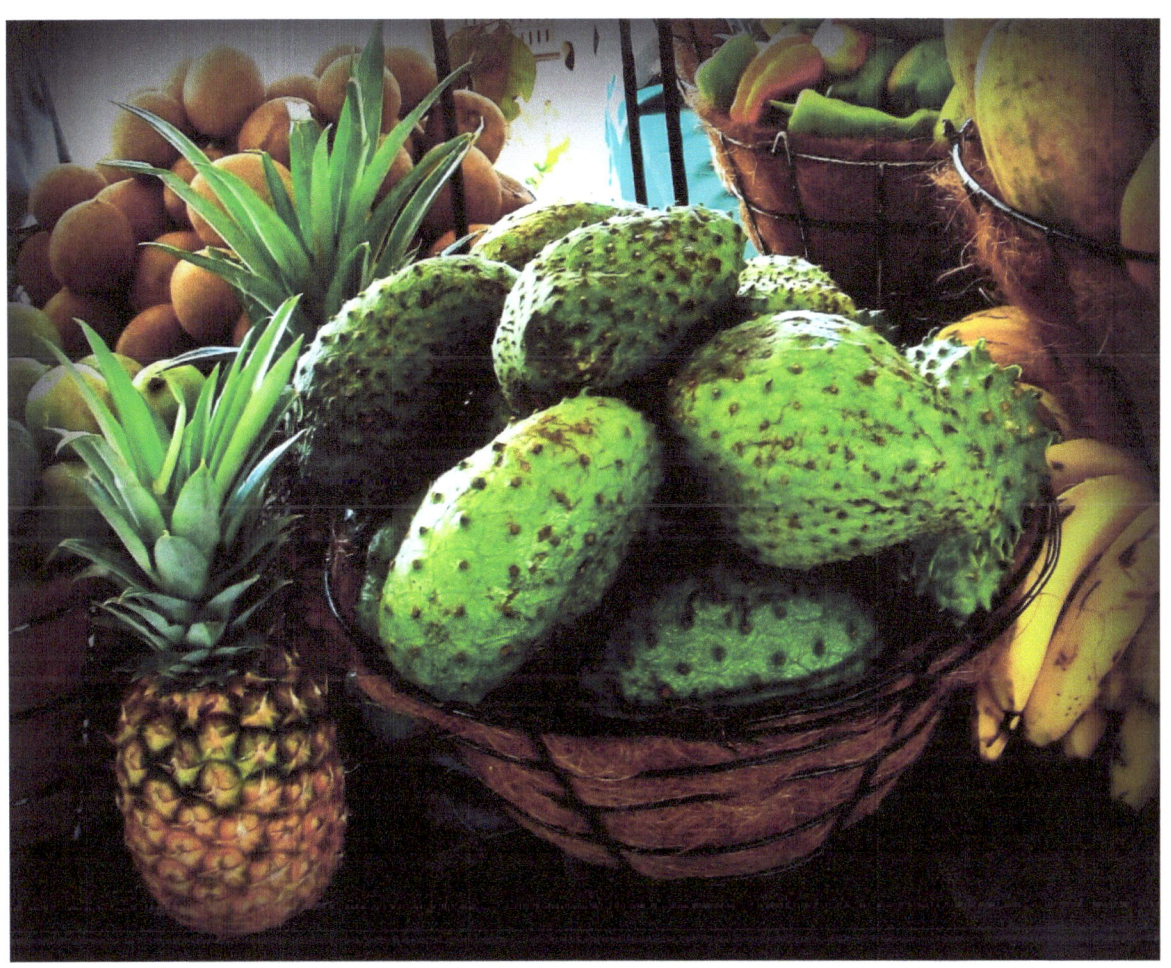

Fruit Market – San Juan

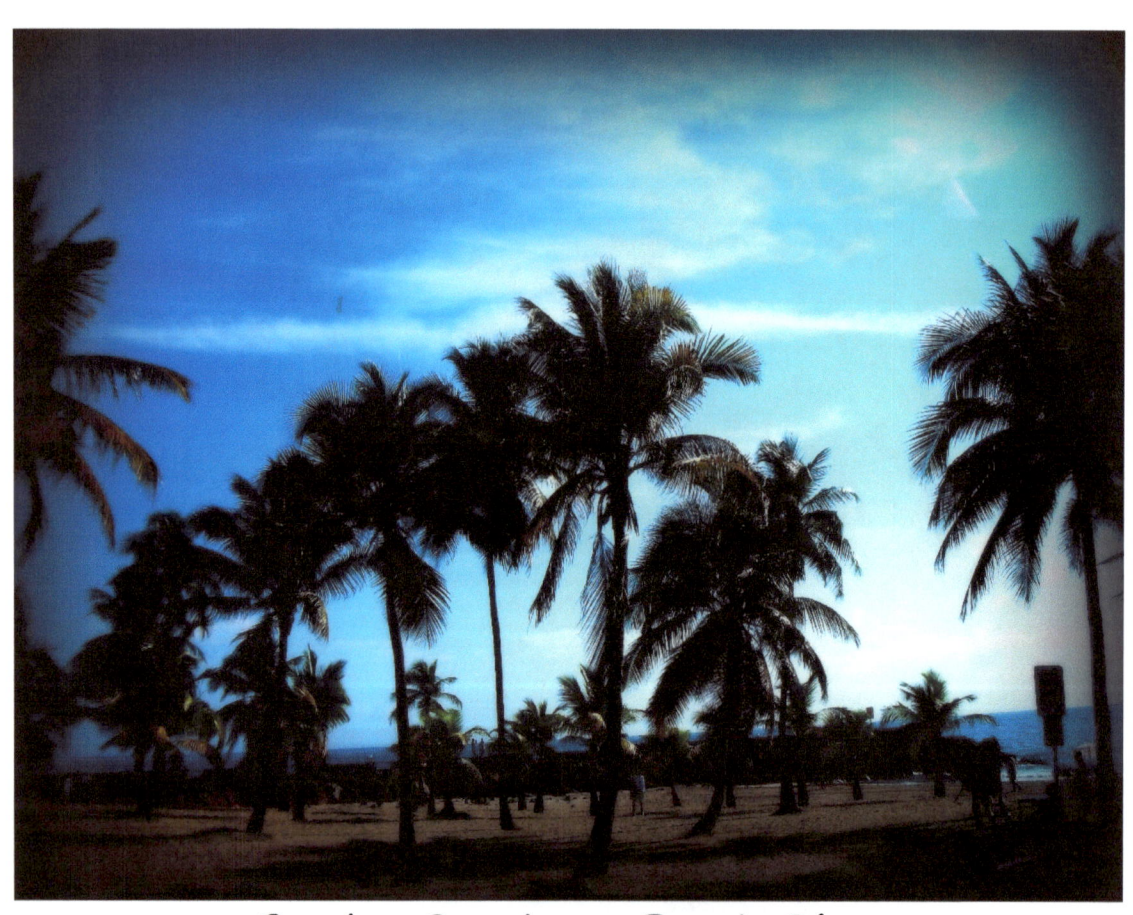

Beach – San Juan, Puerto Rico

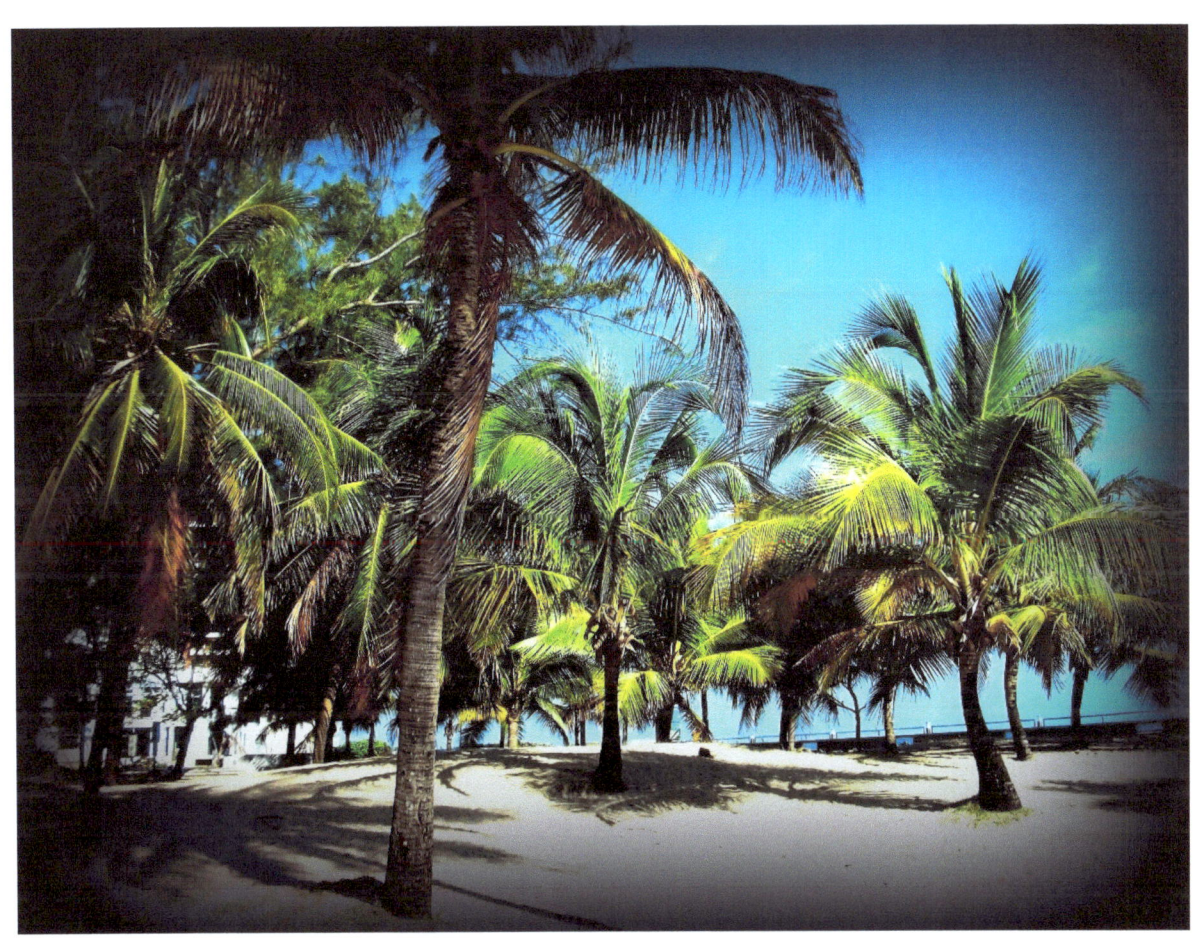

Beach, San Juan

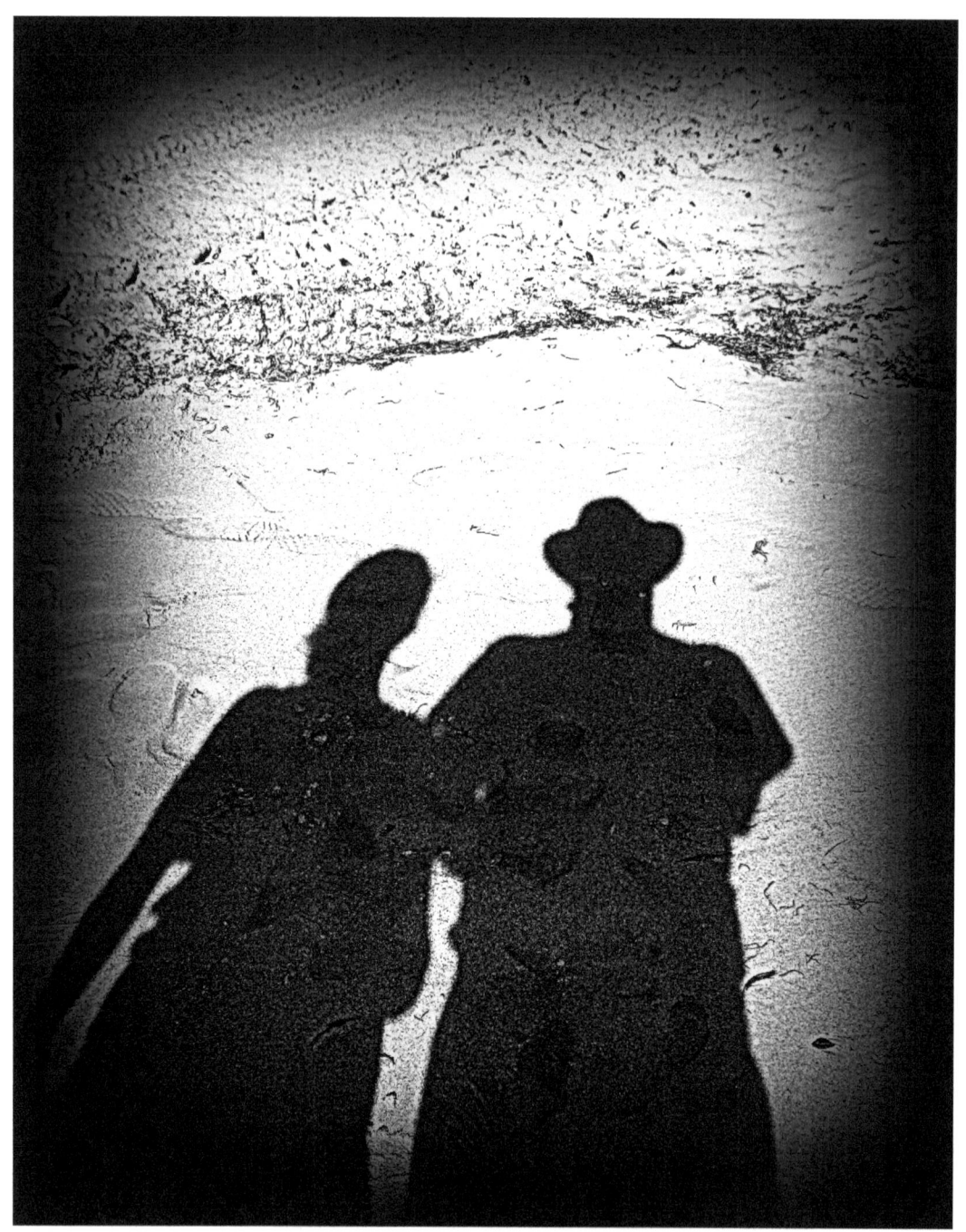

Shadows, Puerto Rico

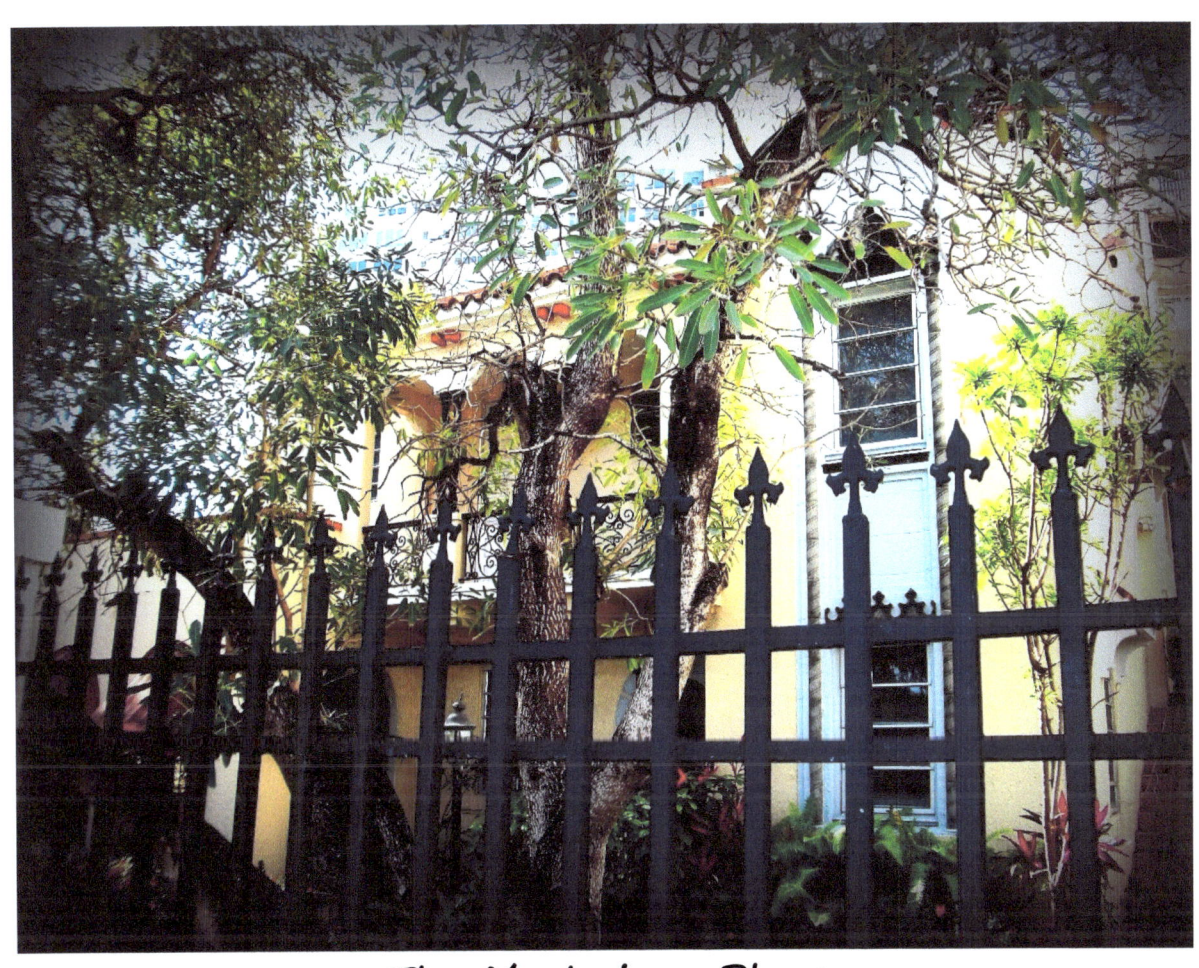

The Mysterious Place

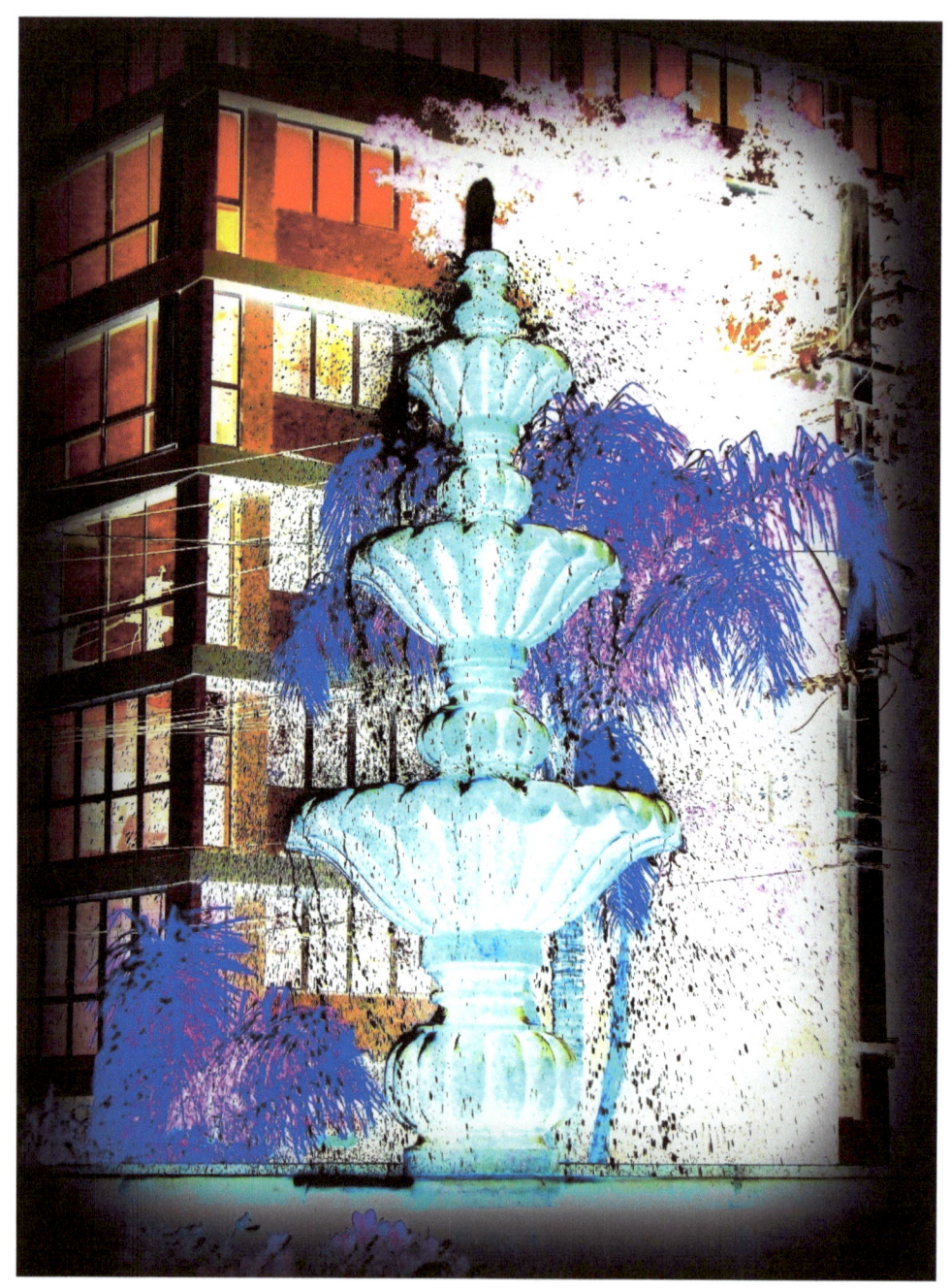

The Fountain

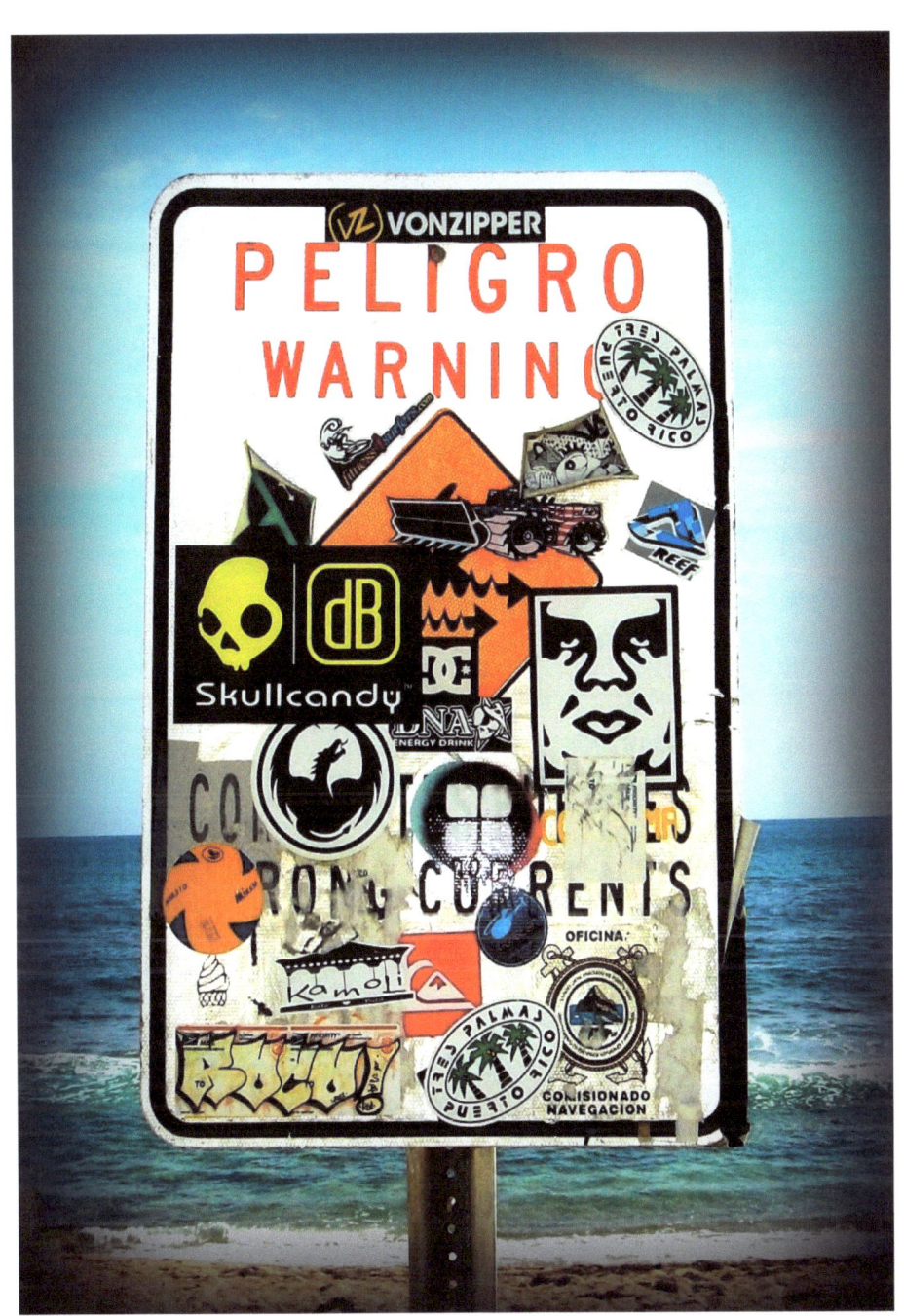

Sign of the Times

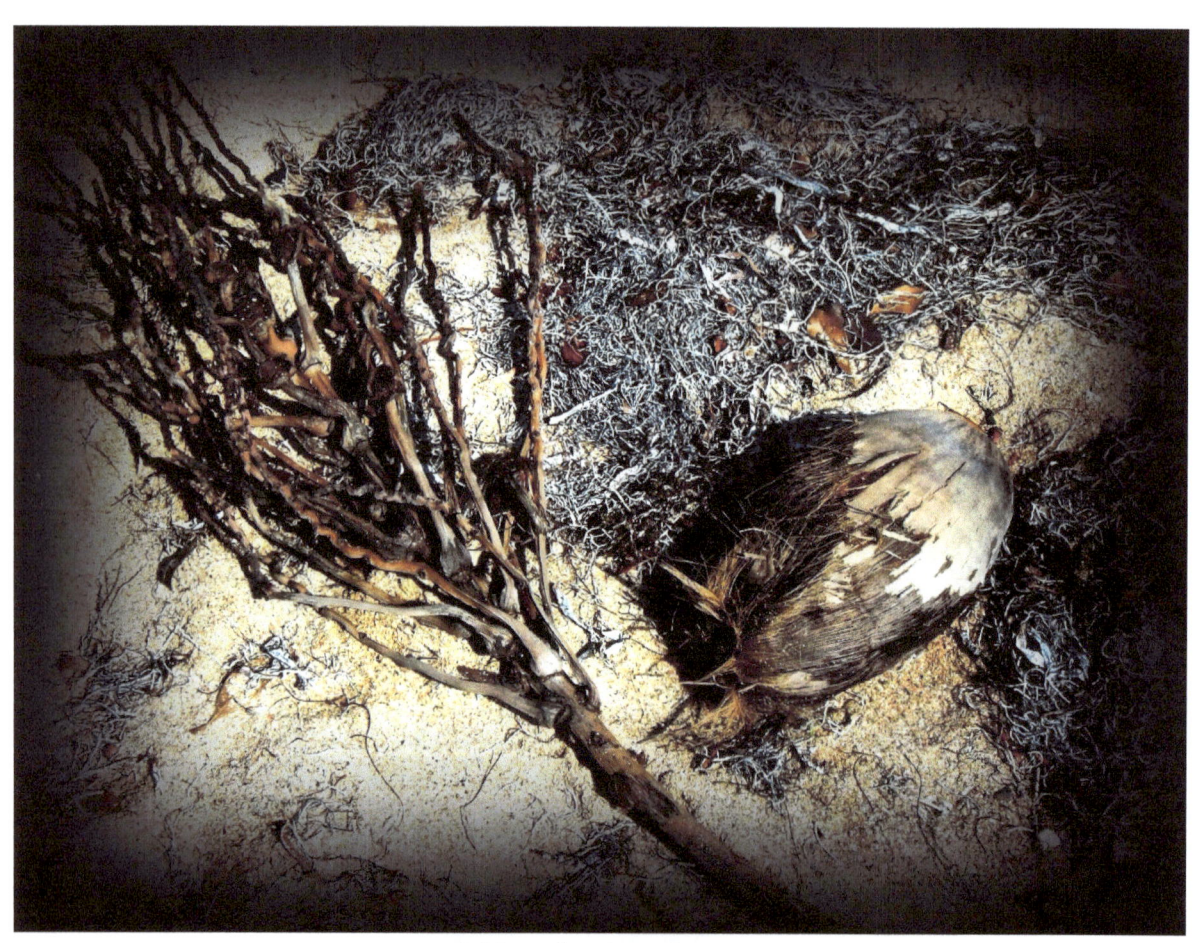

All Washed Up

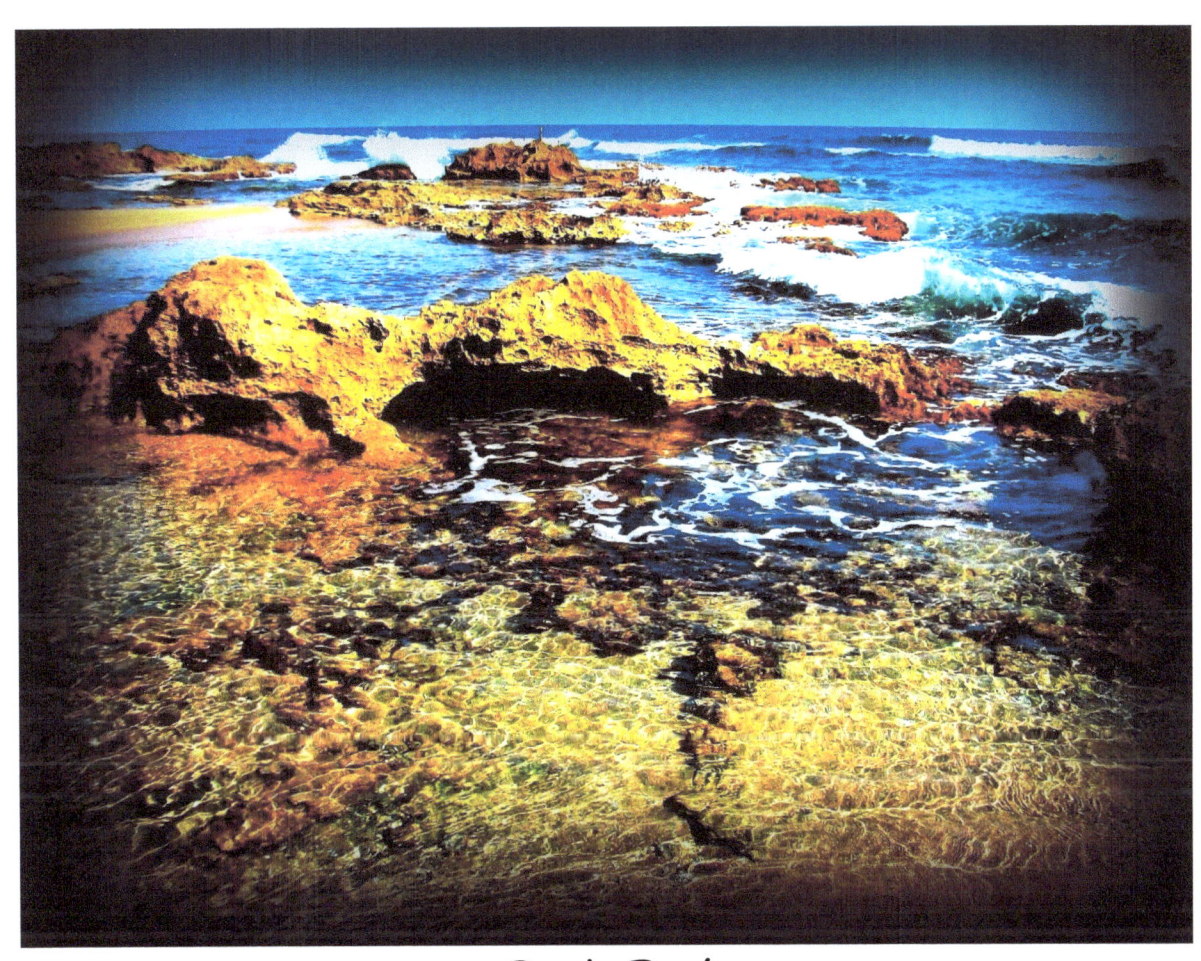

Rock Pool

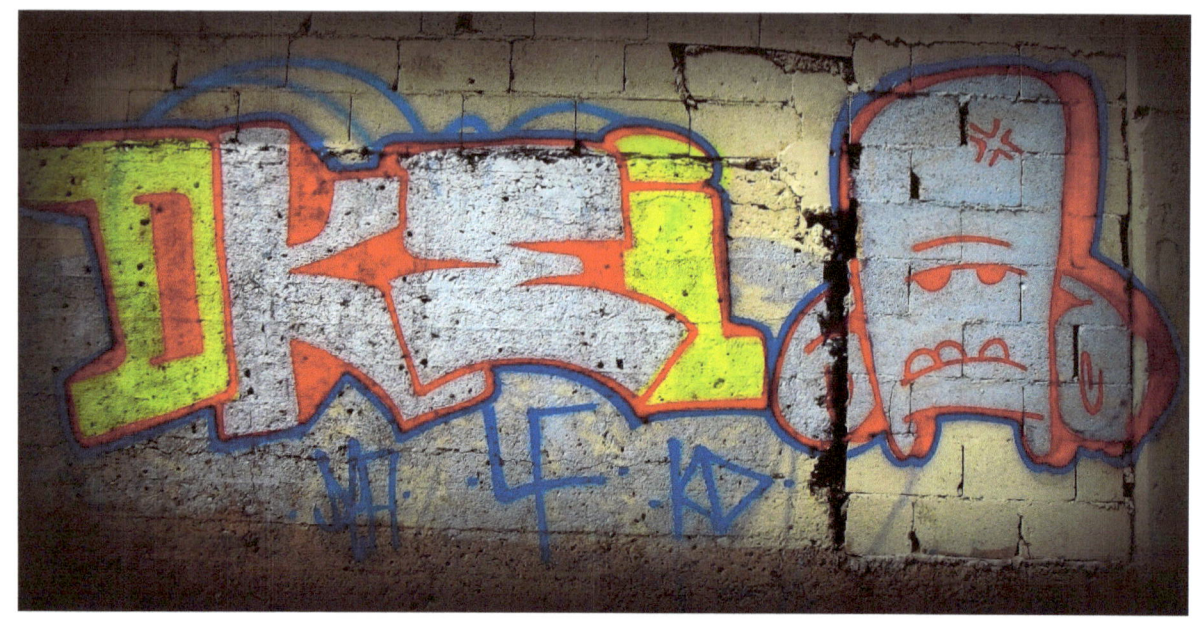

Wall Art

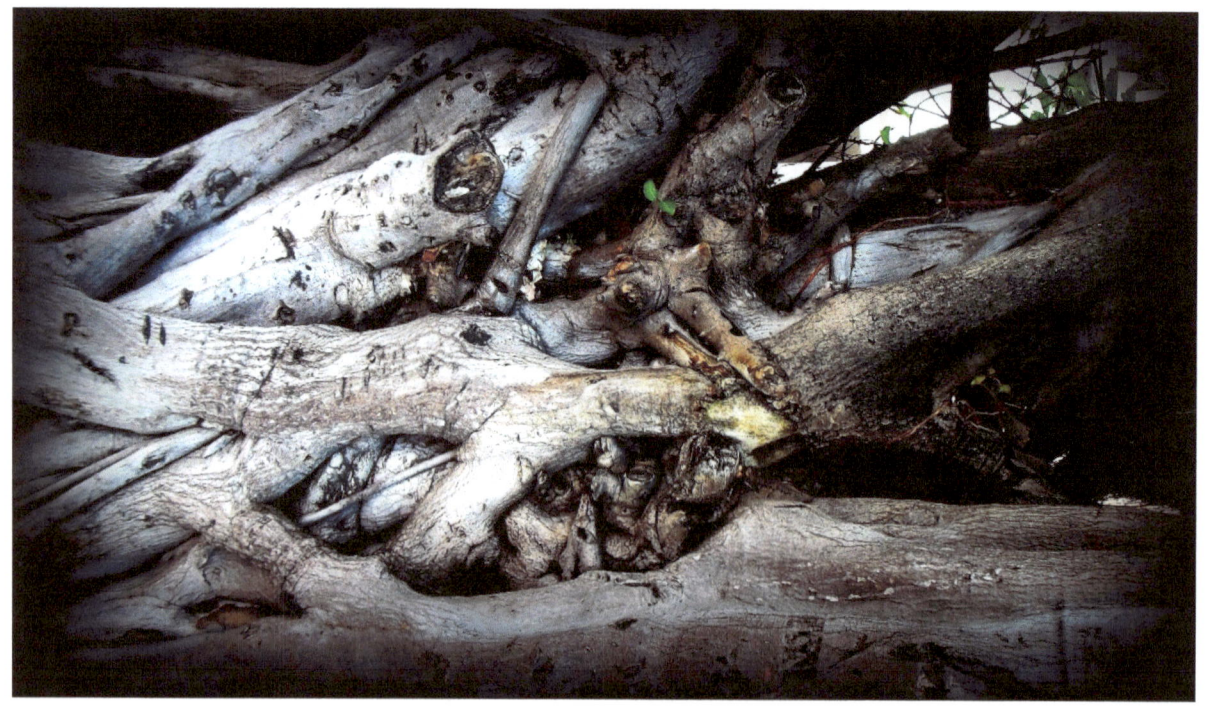

Out on a Limb

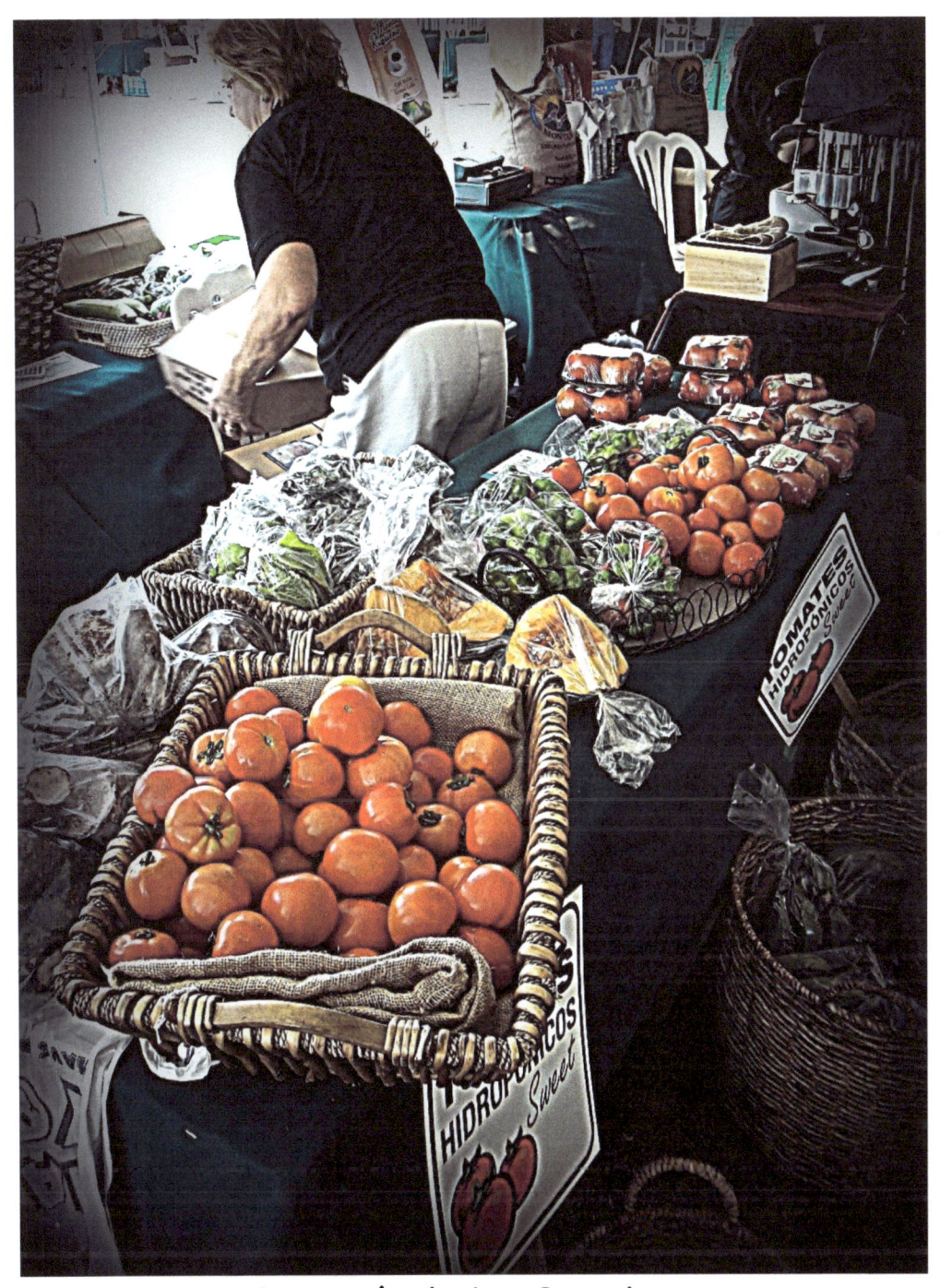

Open Market – San Juan

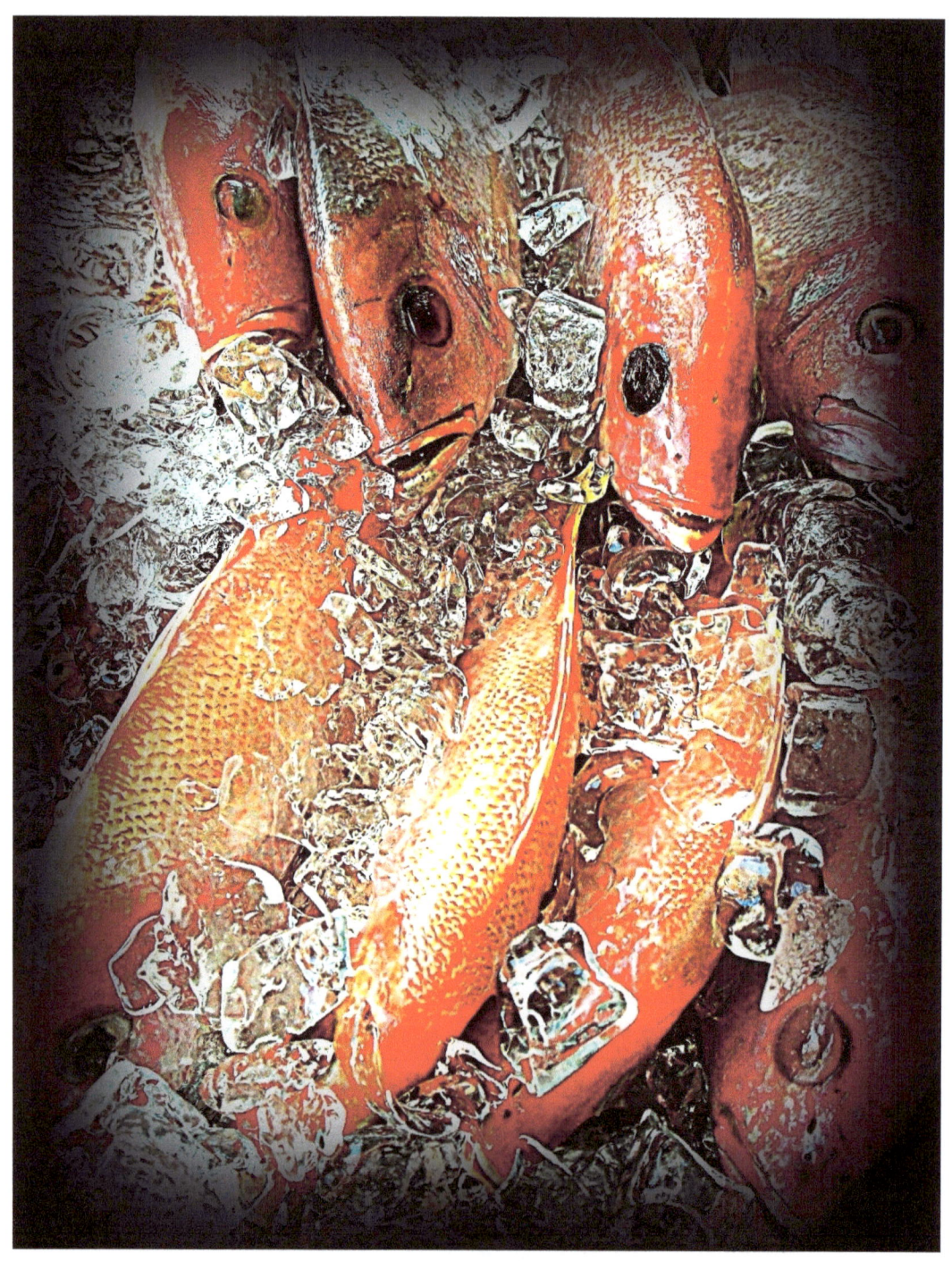

Snapper Snap

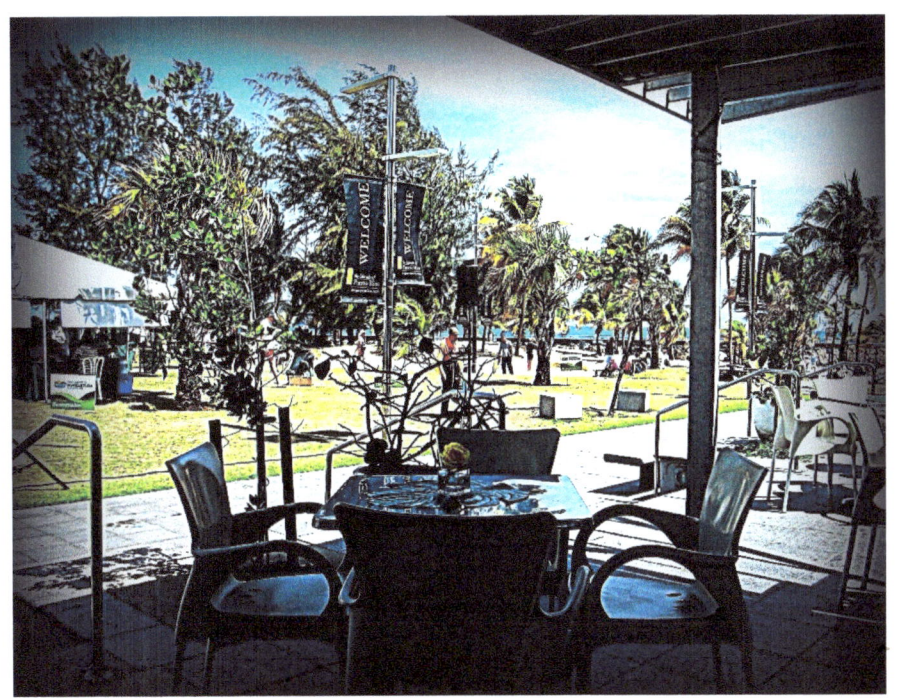

Lunch Time — San Juan

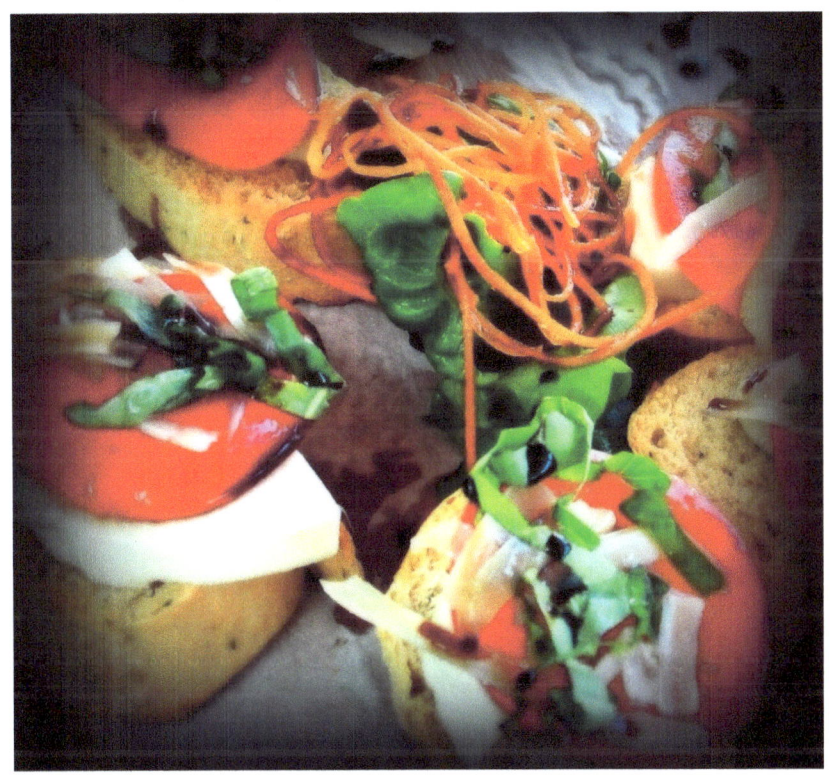

Light Lunch

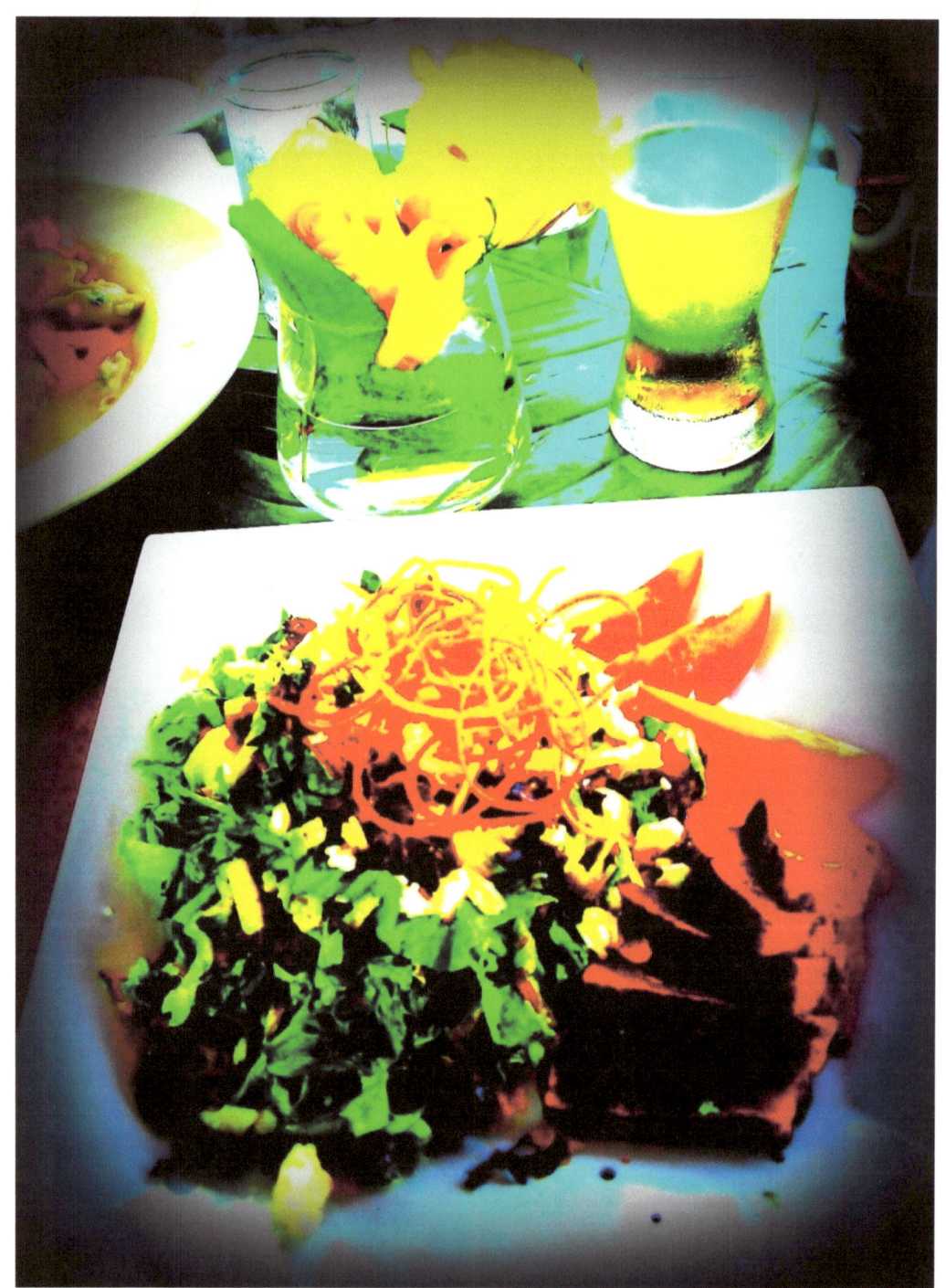

A Little Snack

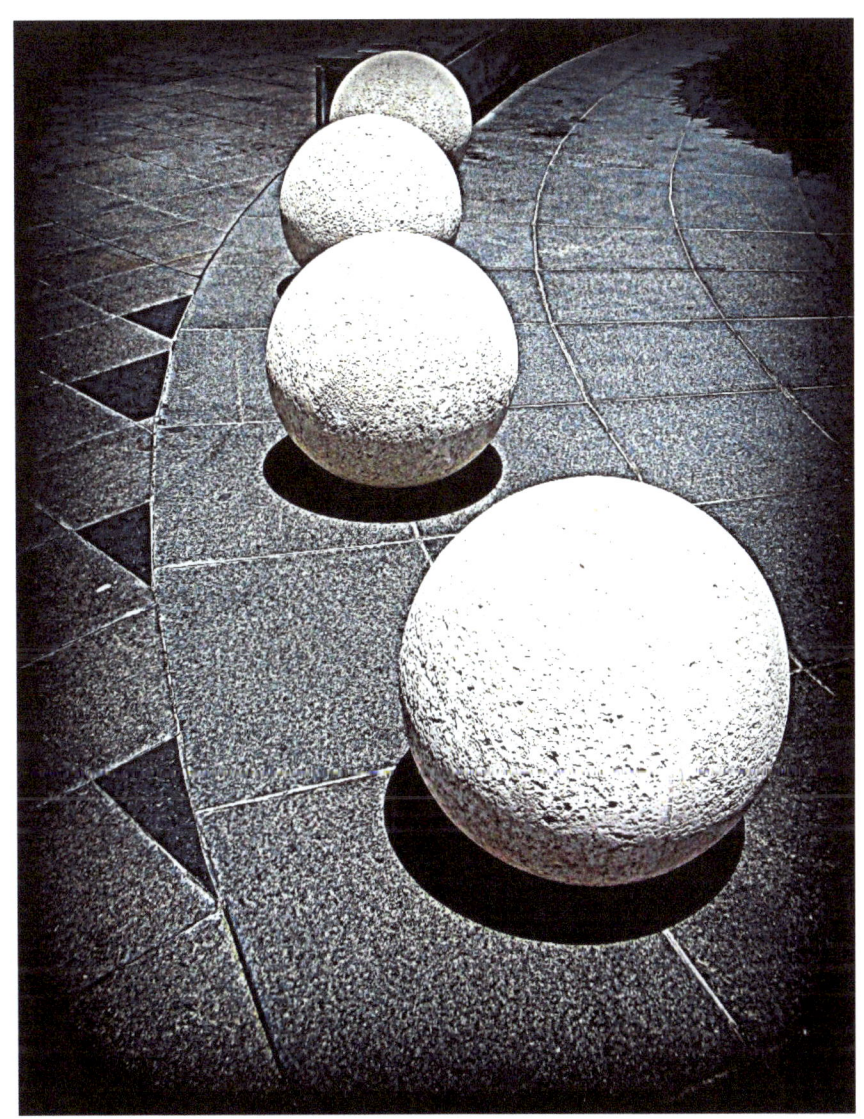

Having a Ball

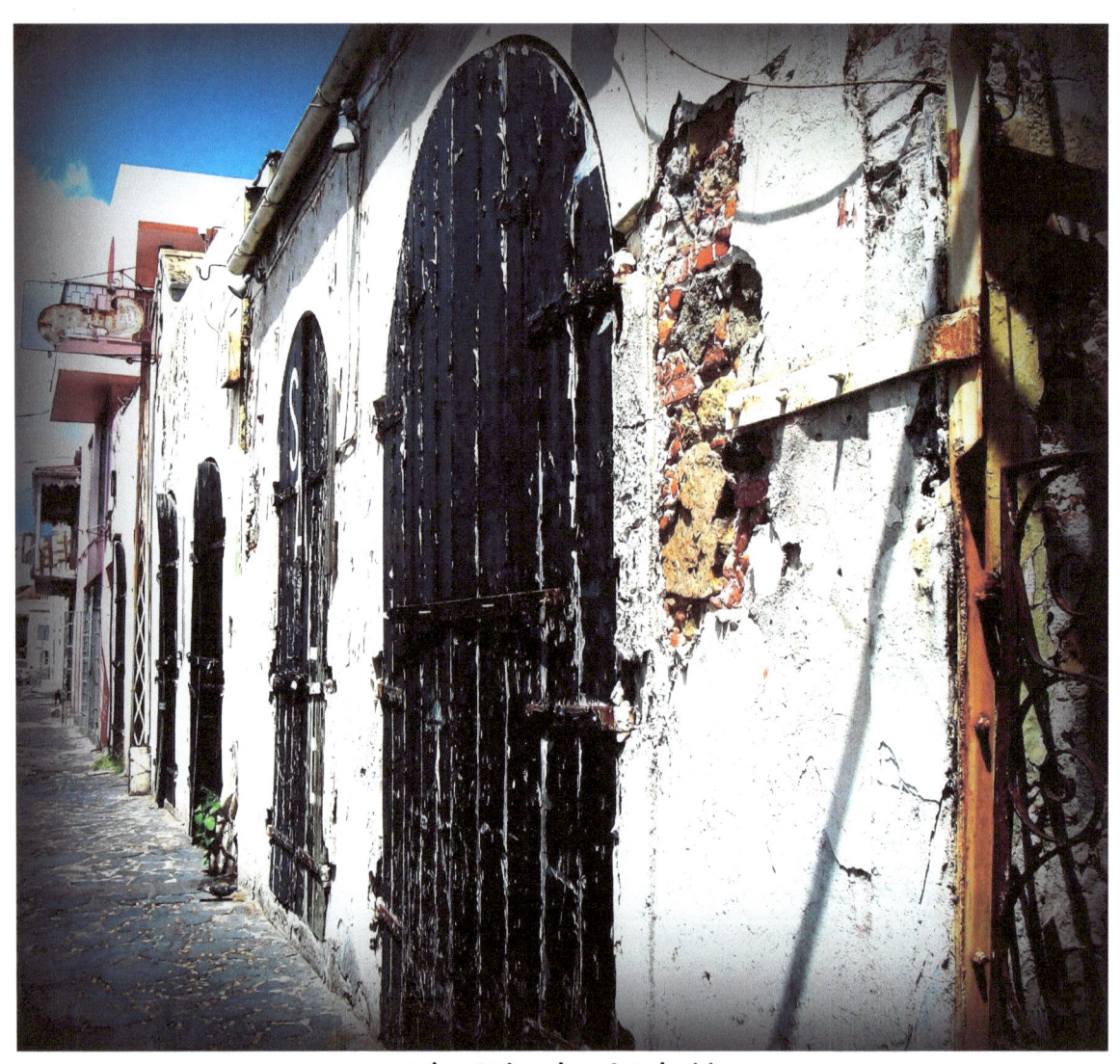

My Kind of Wall

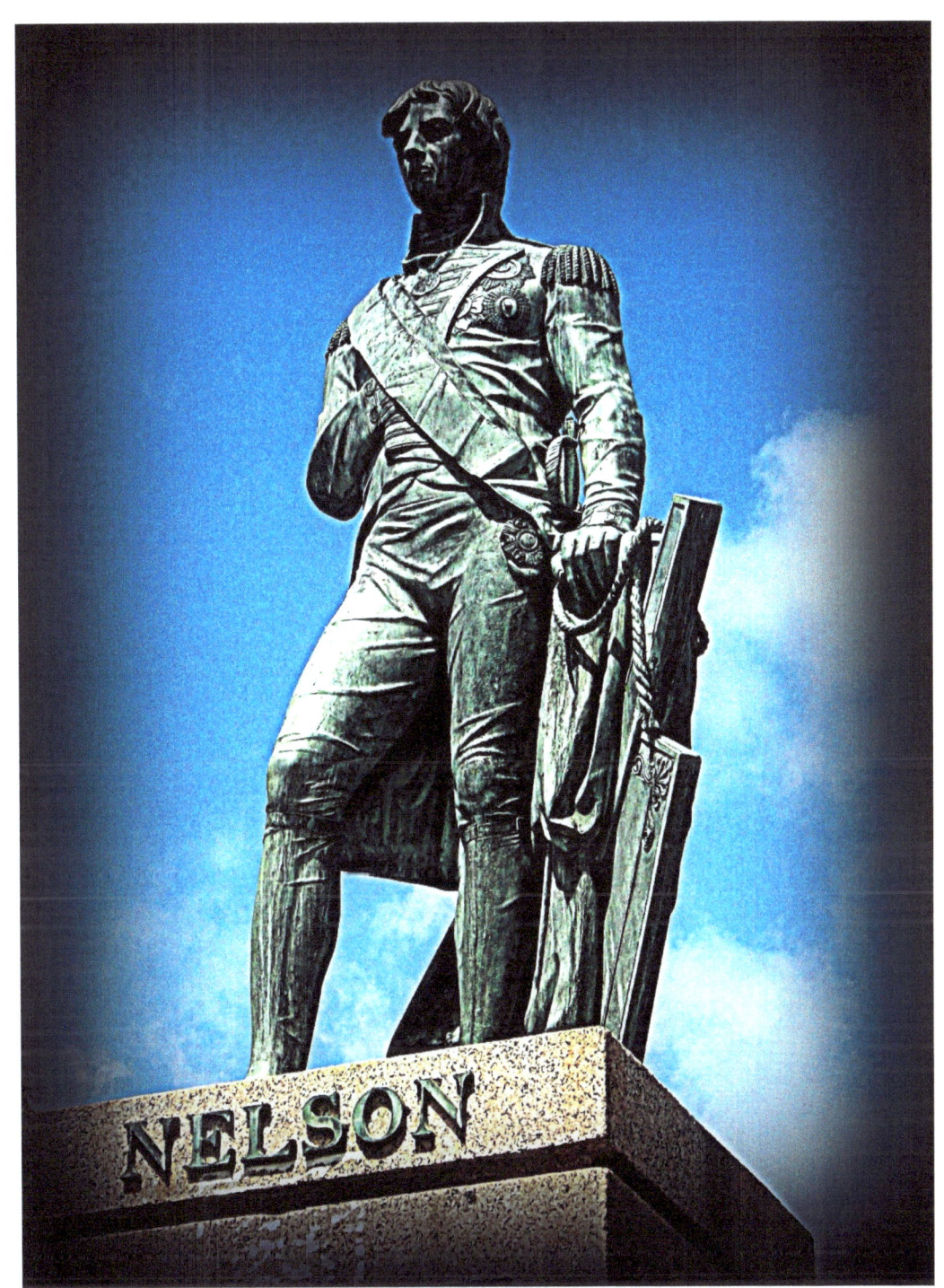

Lord Horatio Nelson

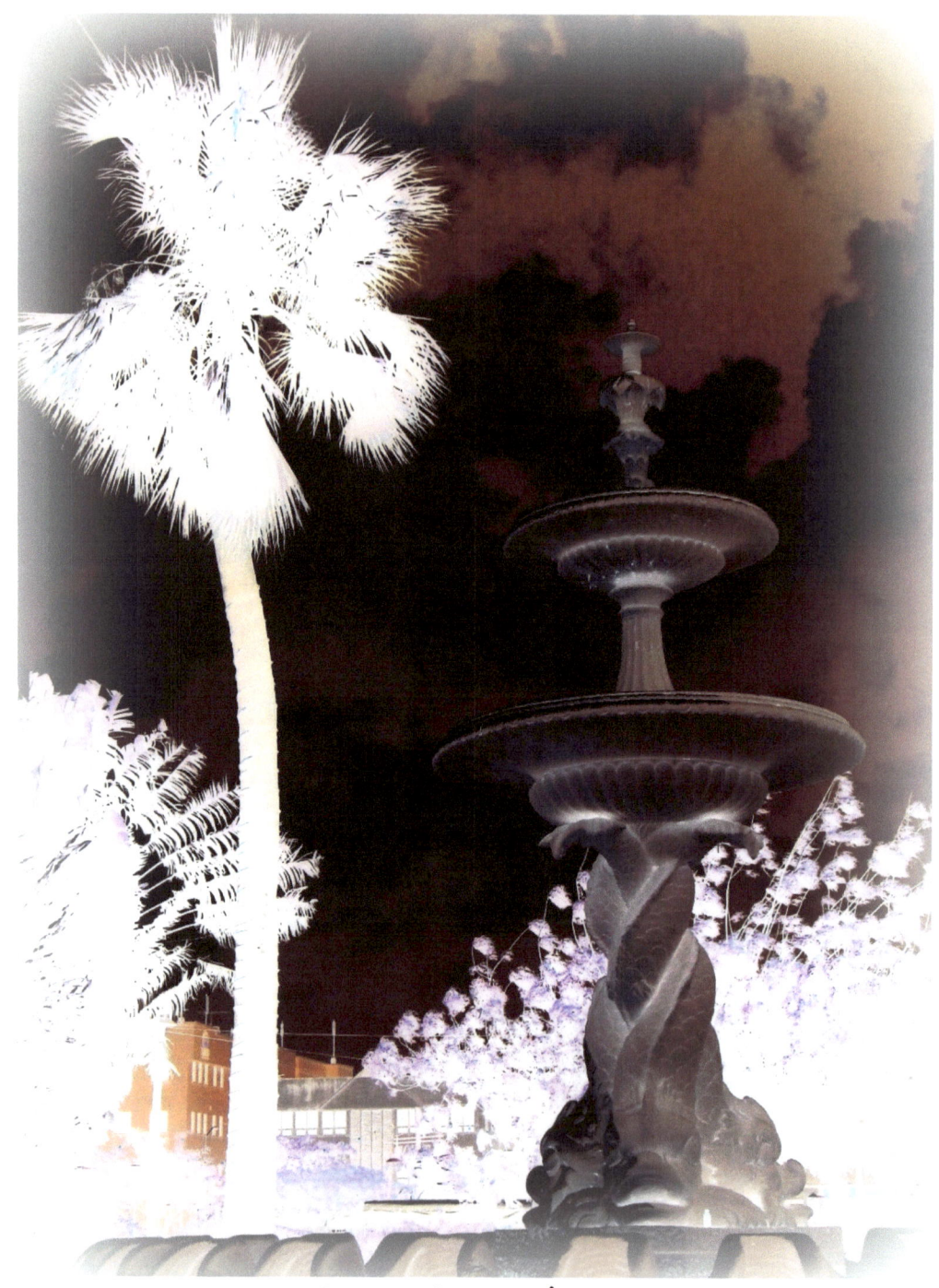

Fountain of Youth

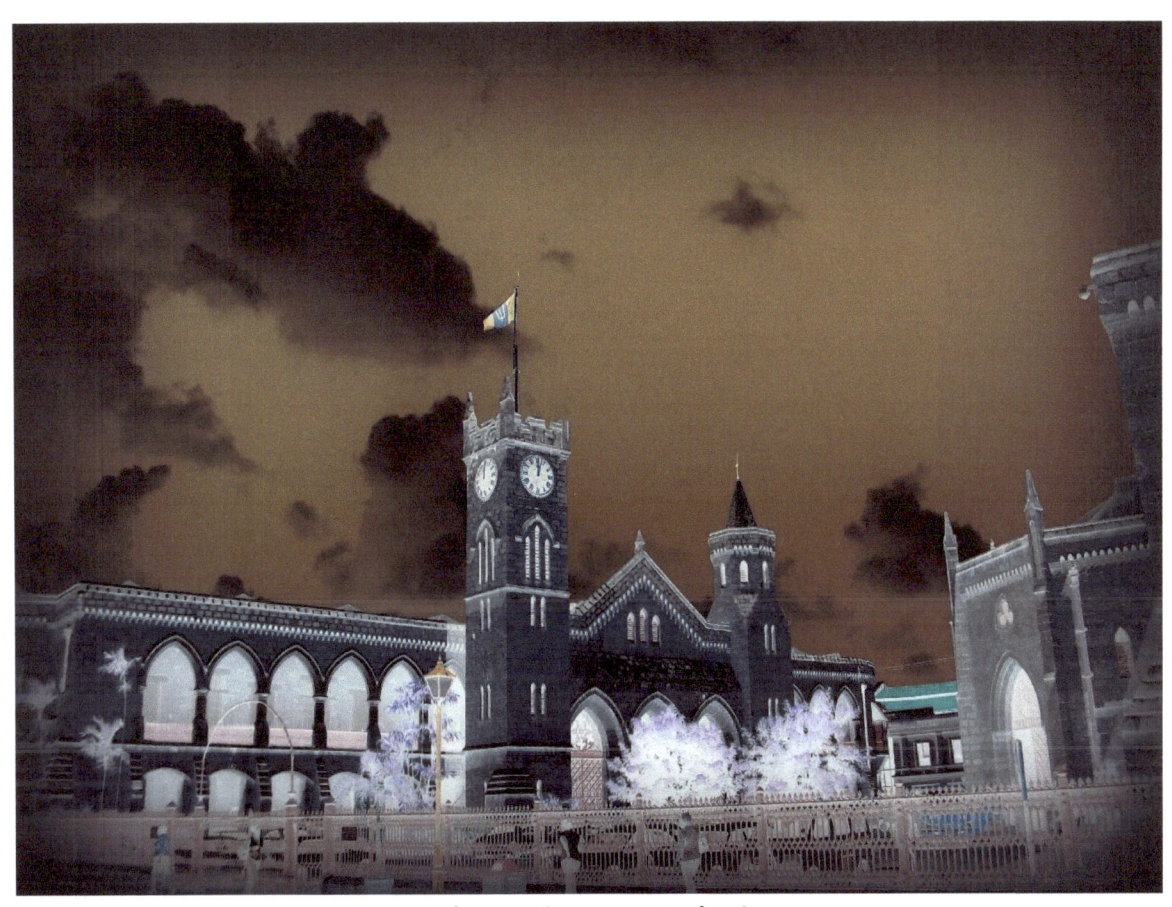

Time for a Drink

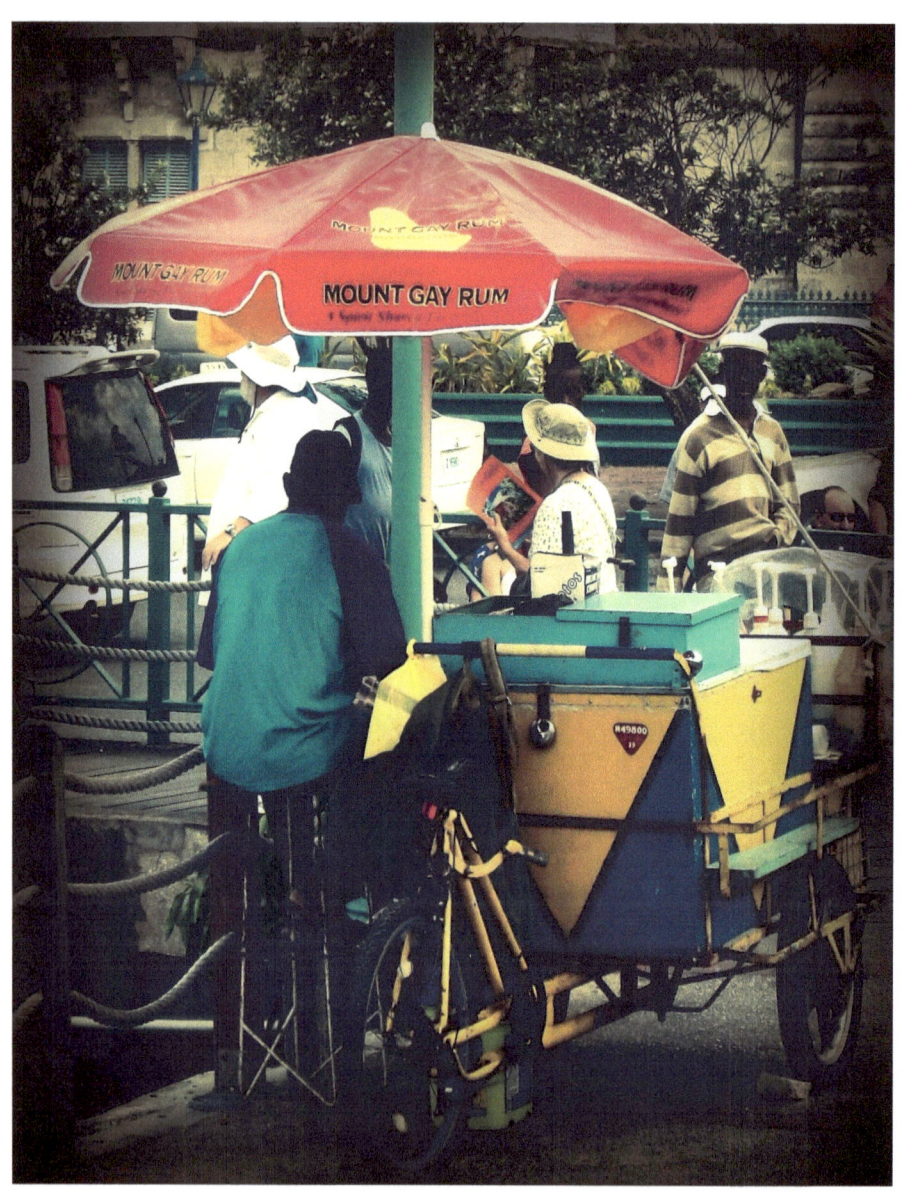

A Rum Business

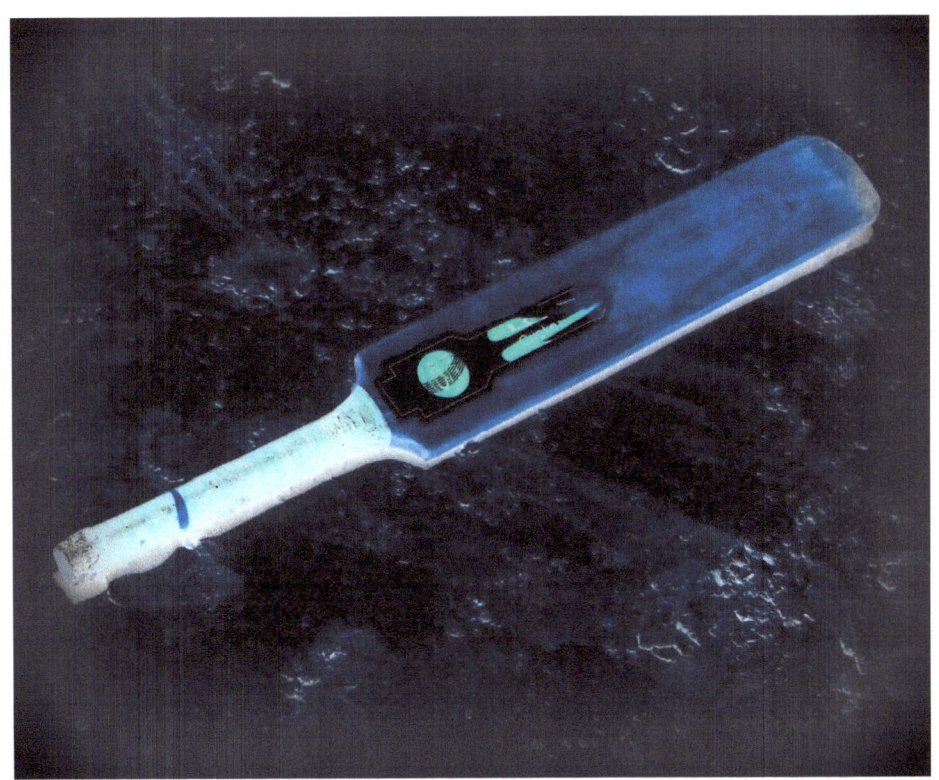

A Rabid Bat

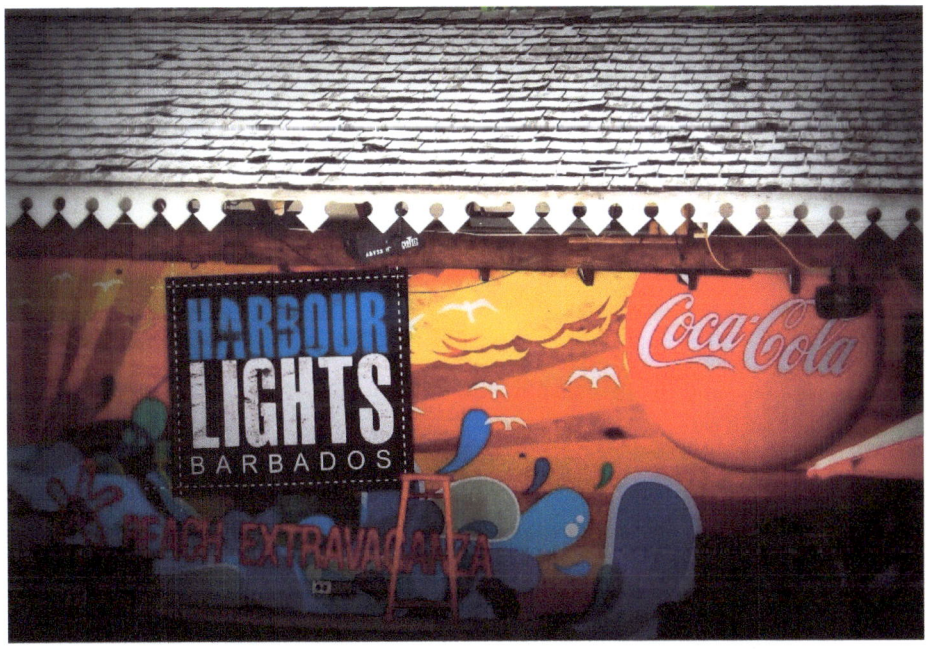

Beach Extravaganza — Barbados

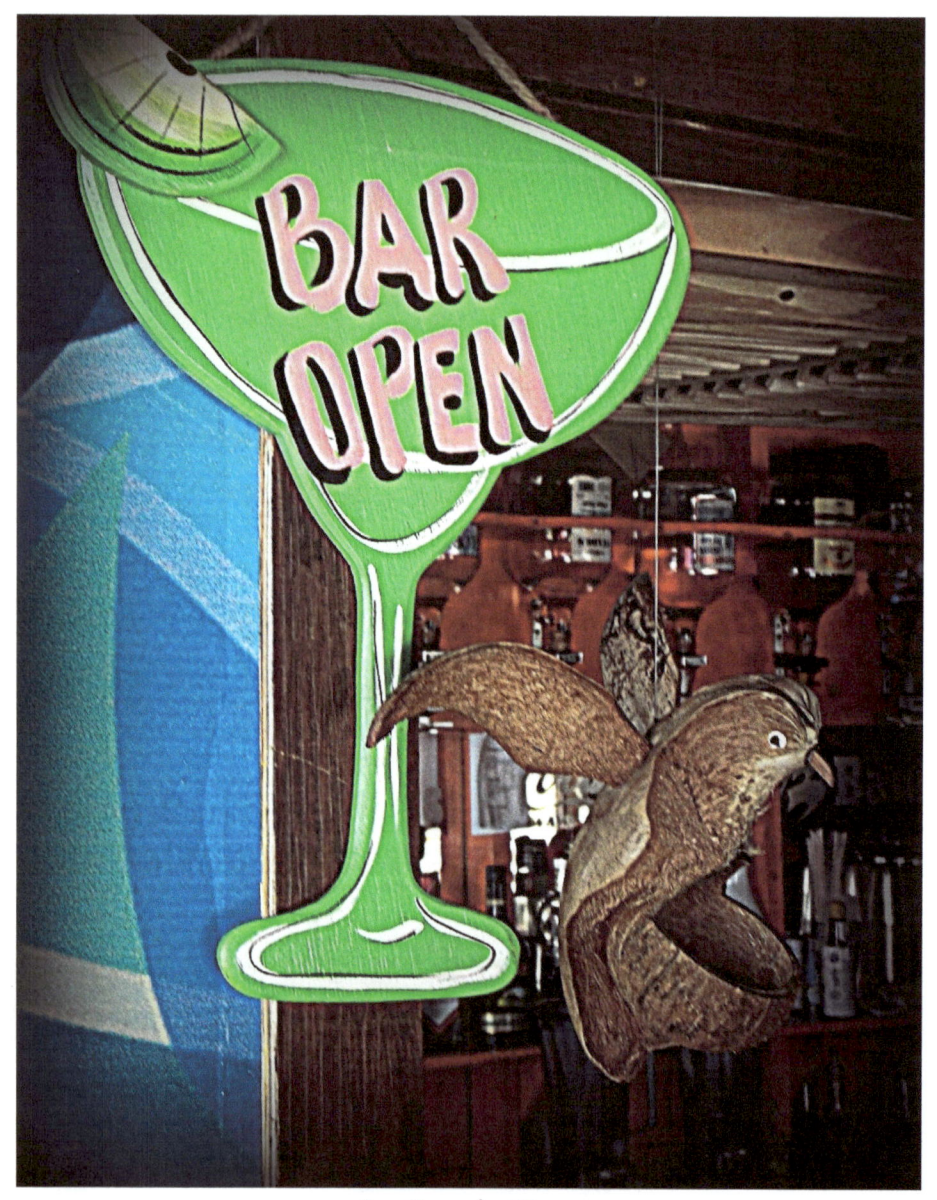

A Good Sign

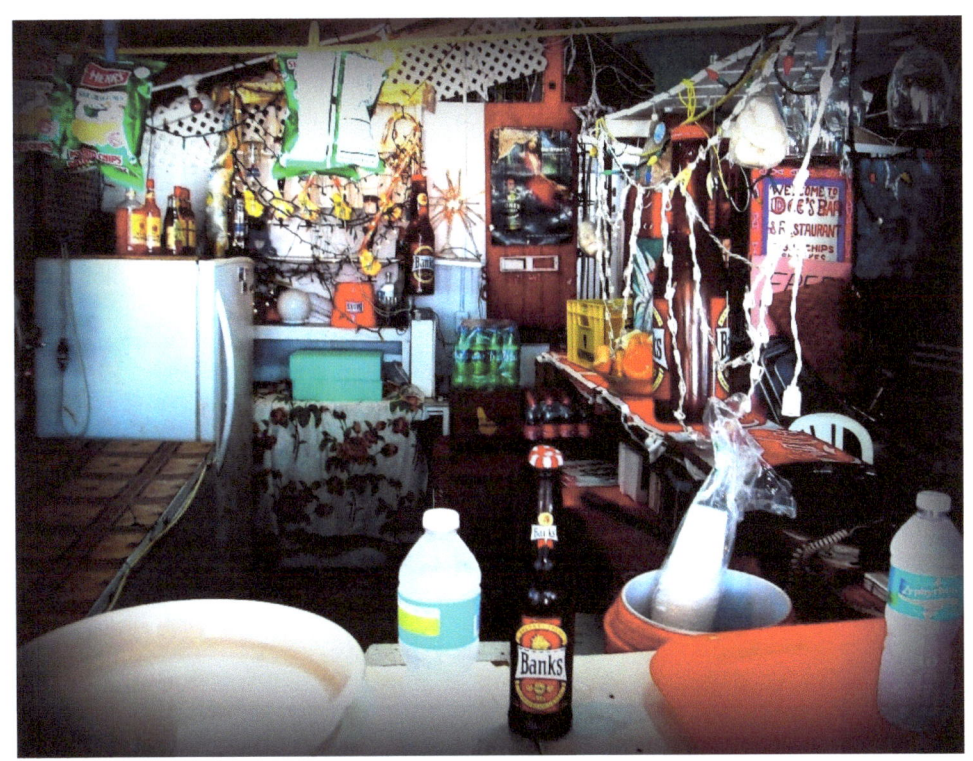

Best Fried Fish in Town

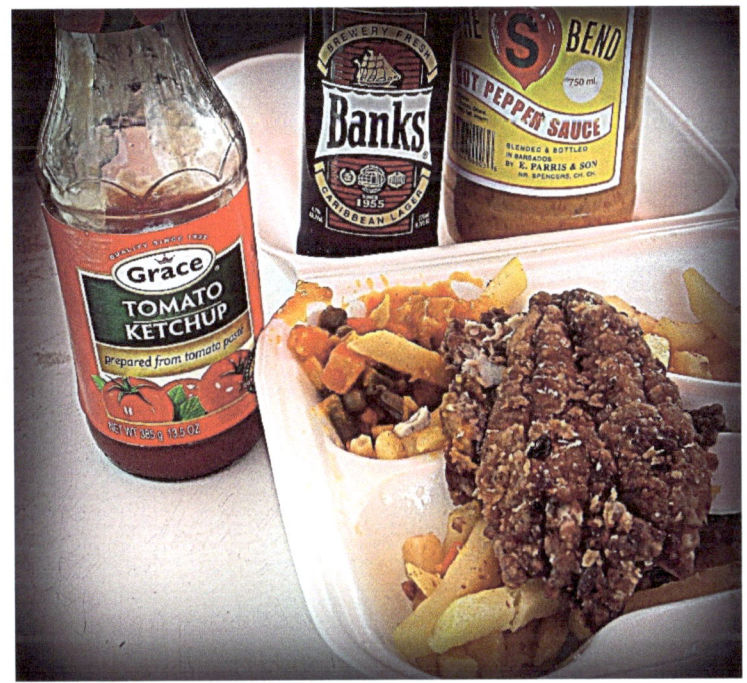

I Told You!

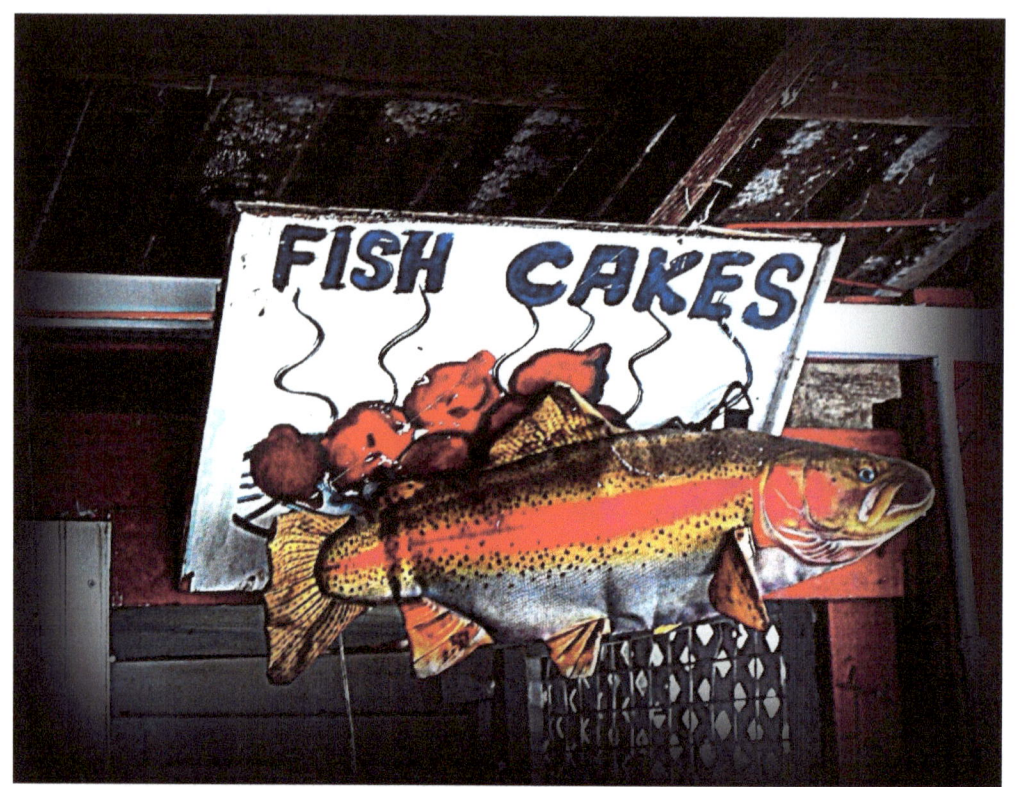

Fishy Business

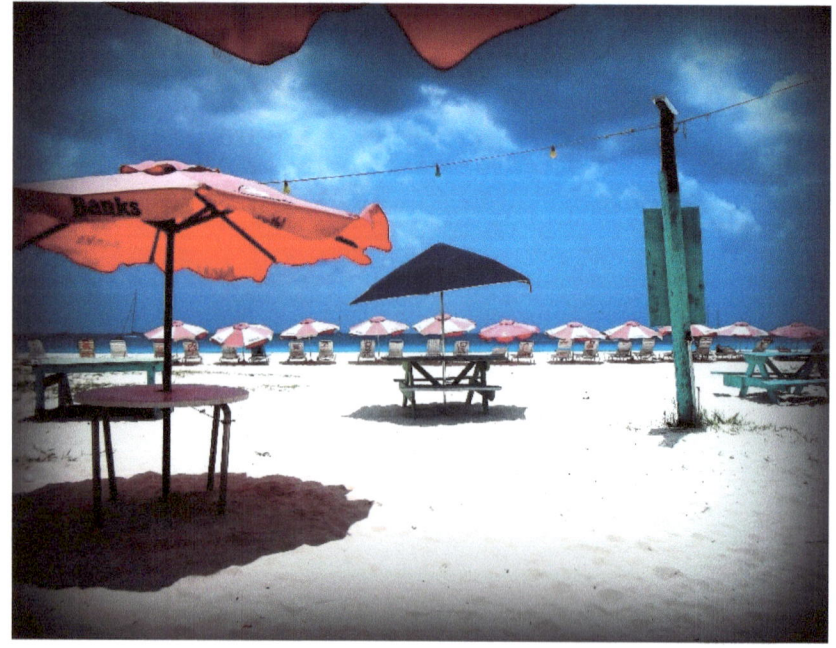

Life's a ....

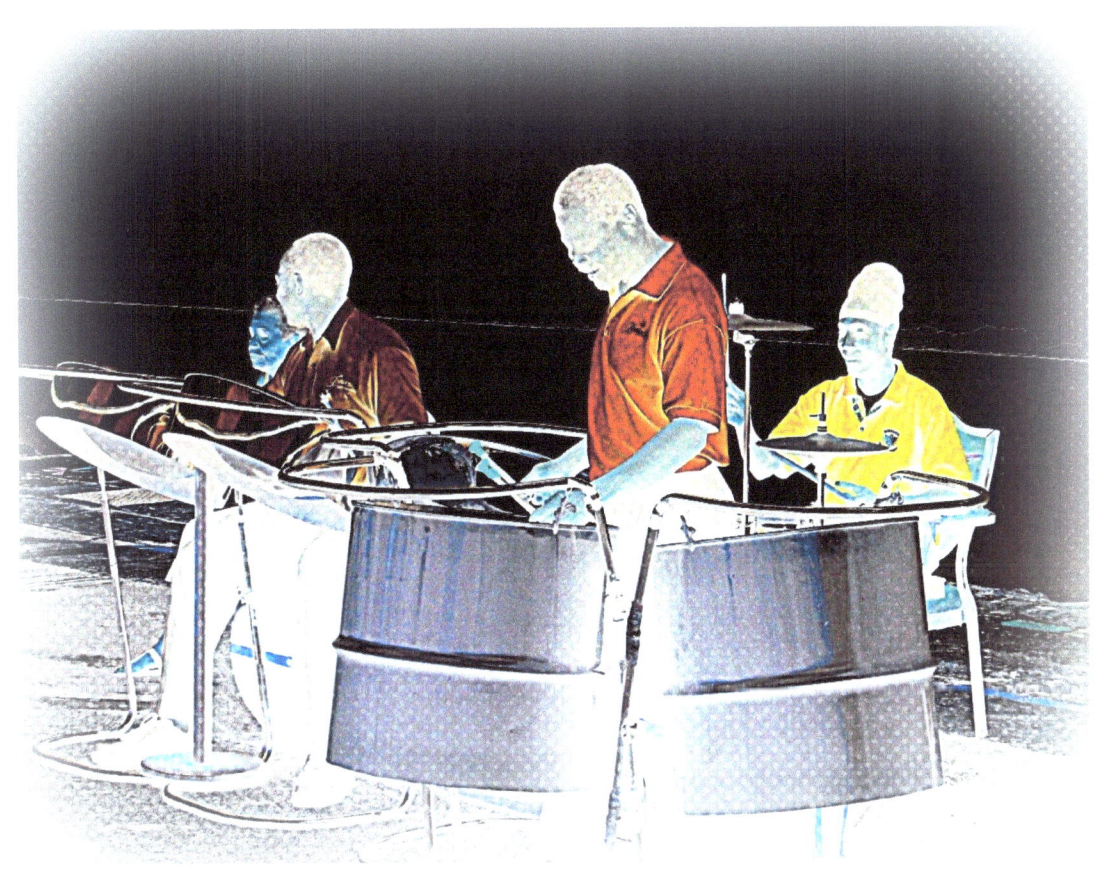

Steeling the Show

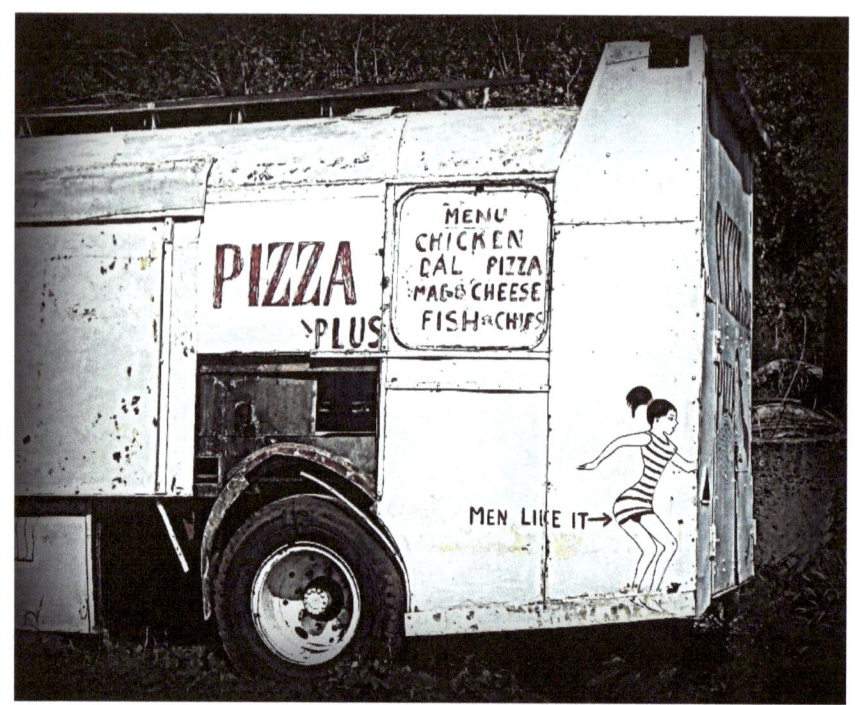

Pizza Plus........

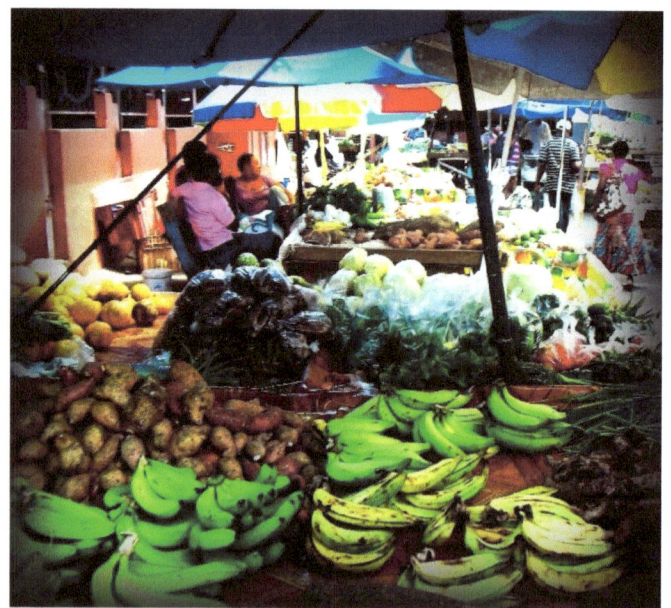

Fruit Market

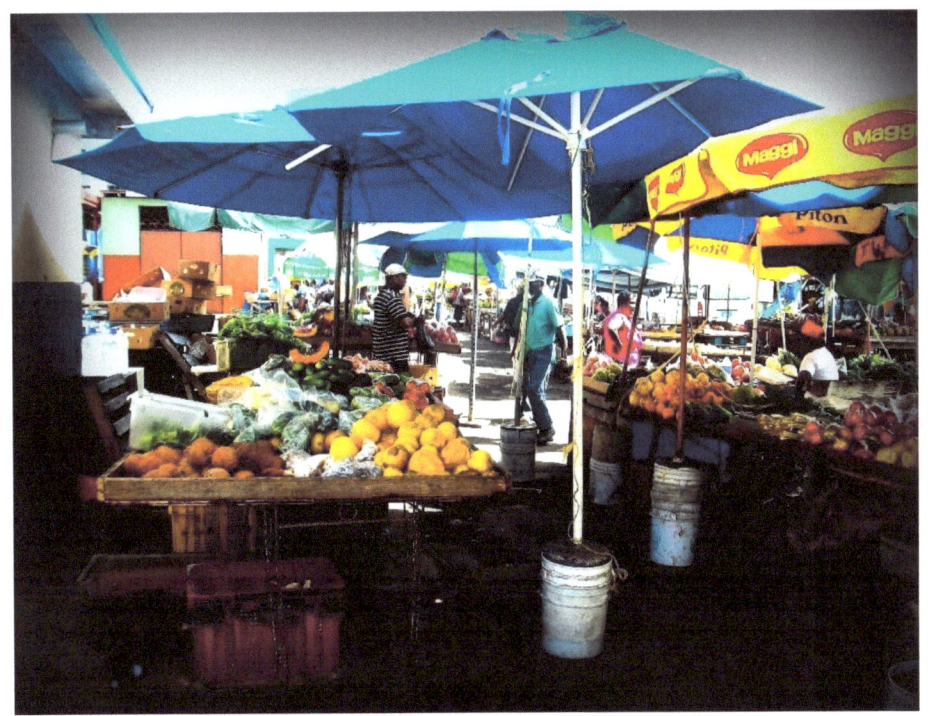

More fruit

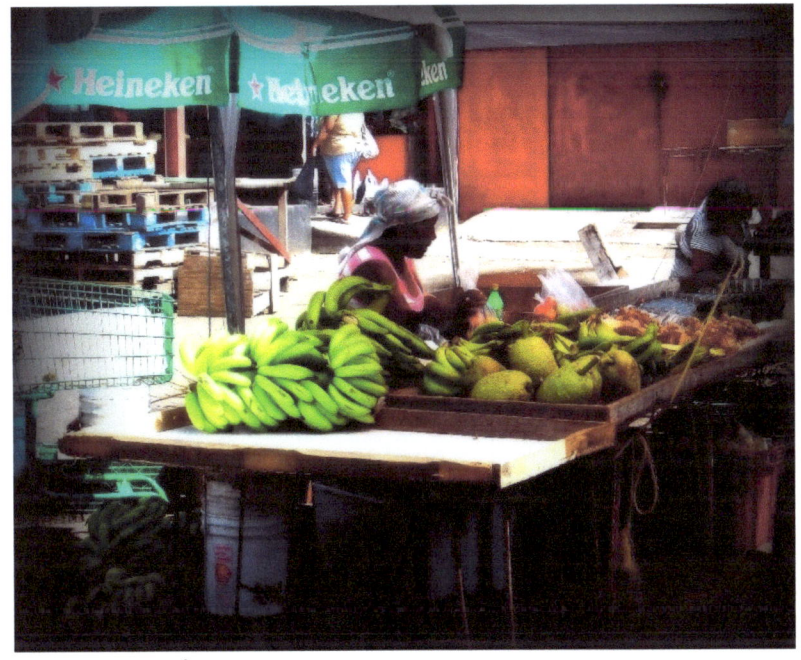

Yes, we have no Bananas

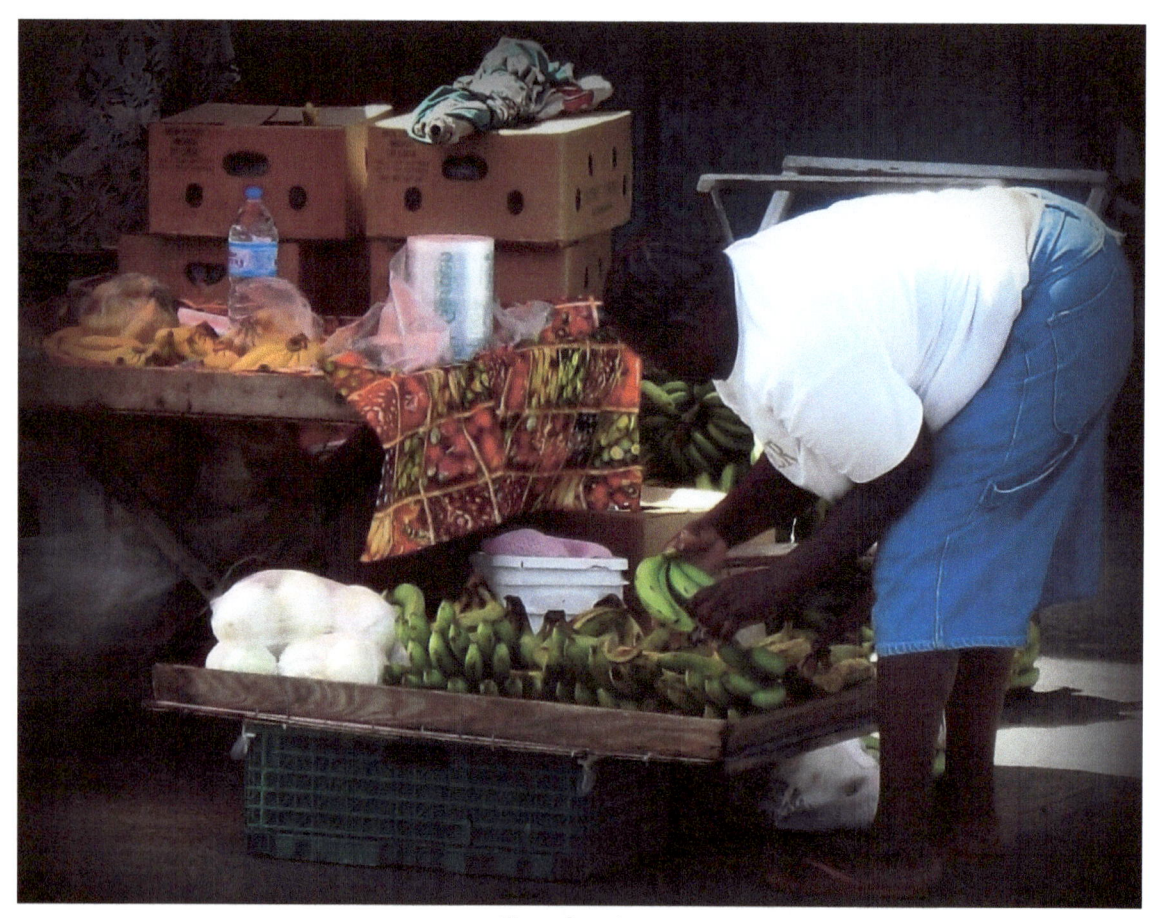

Perfect....

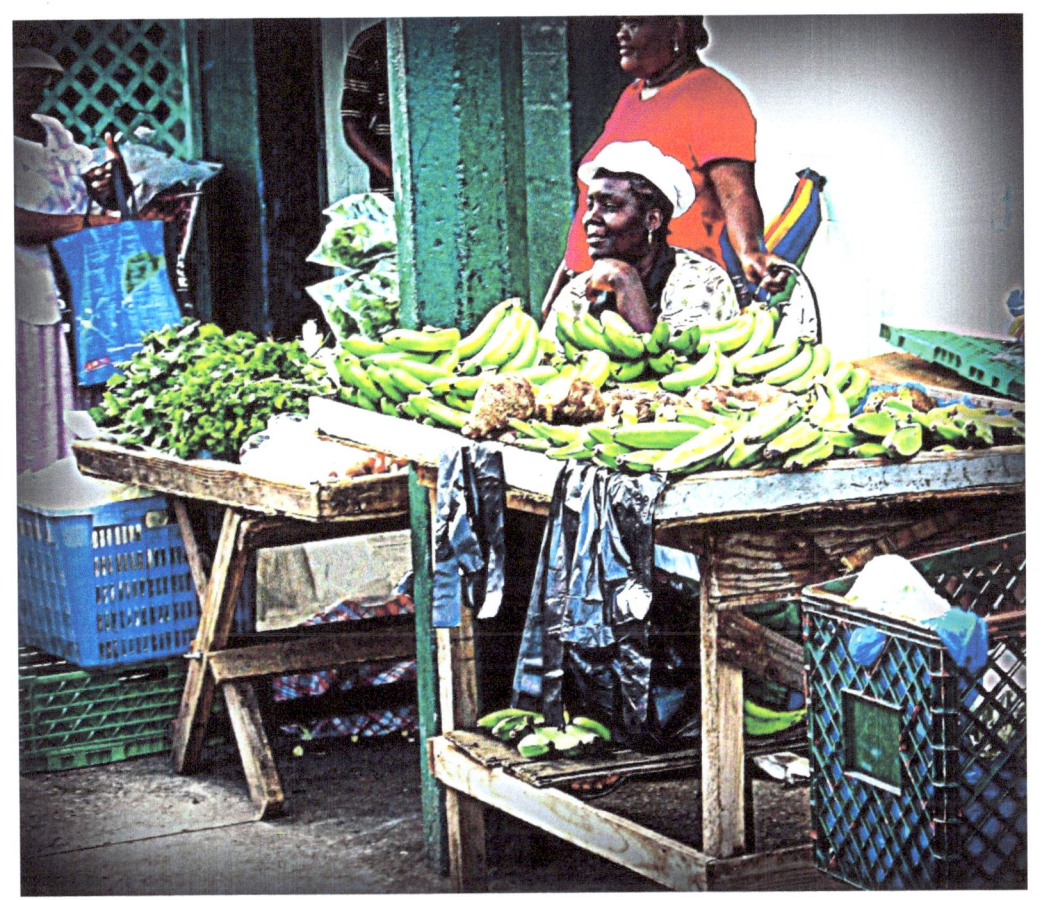

Fruit Seller – Barbados

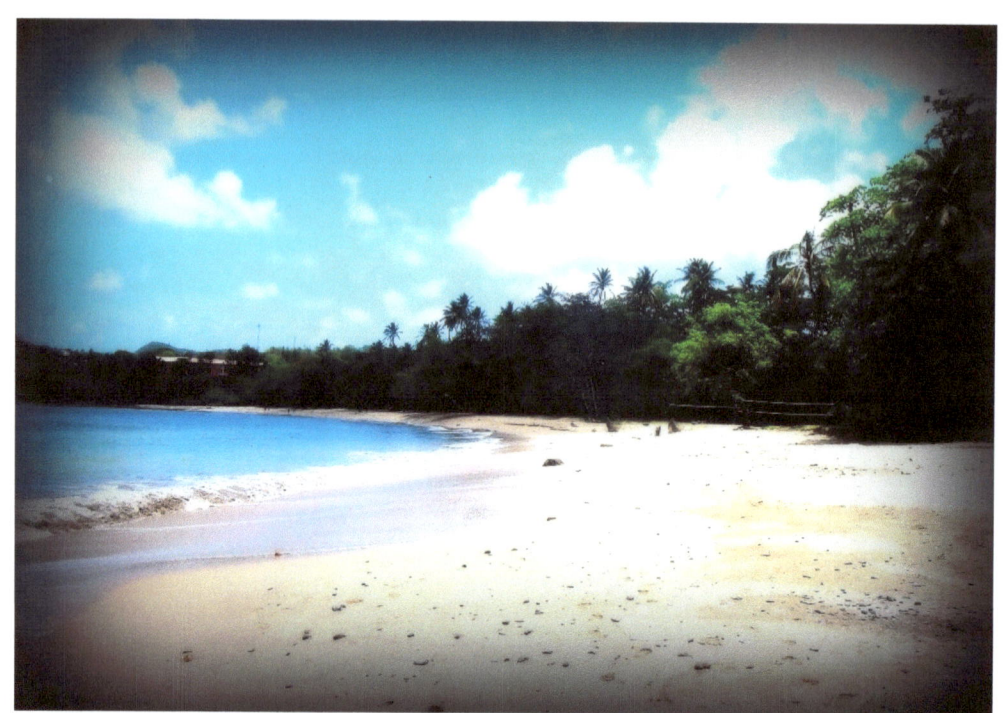

St. Lucia

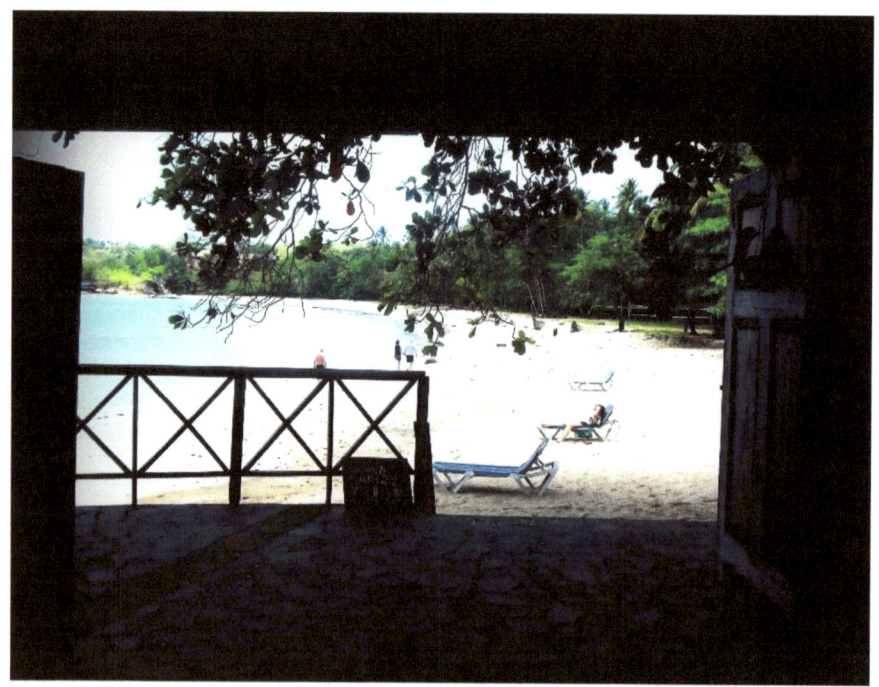

St. Lucia II

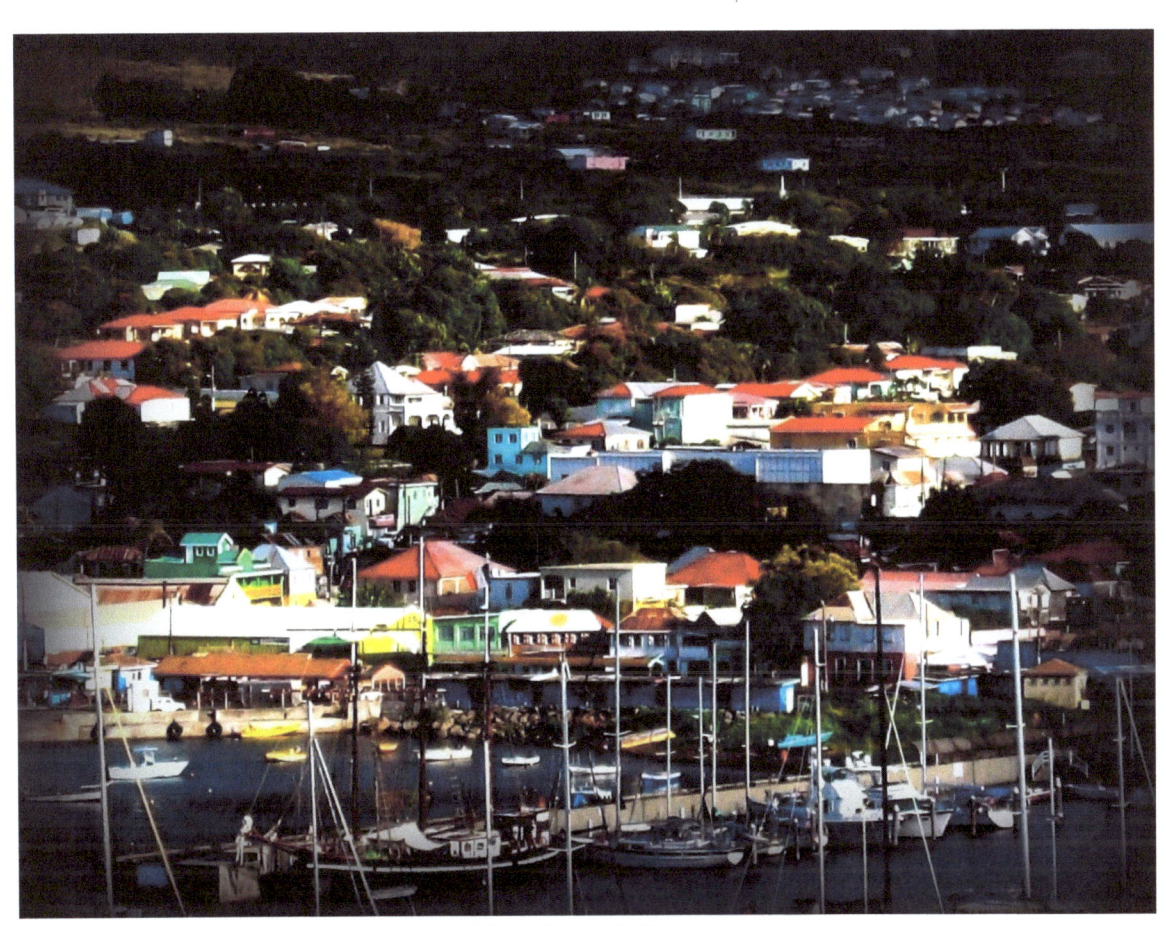

Harbor View

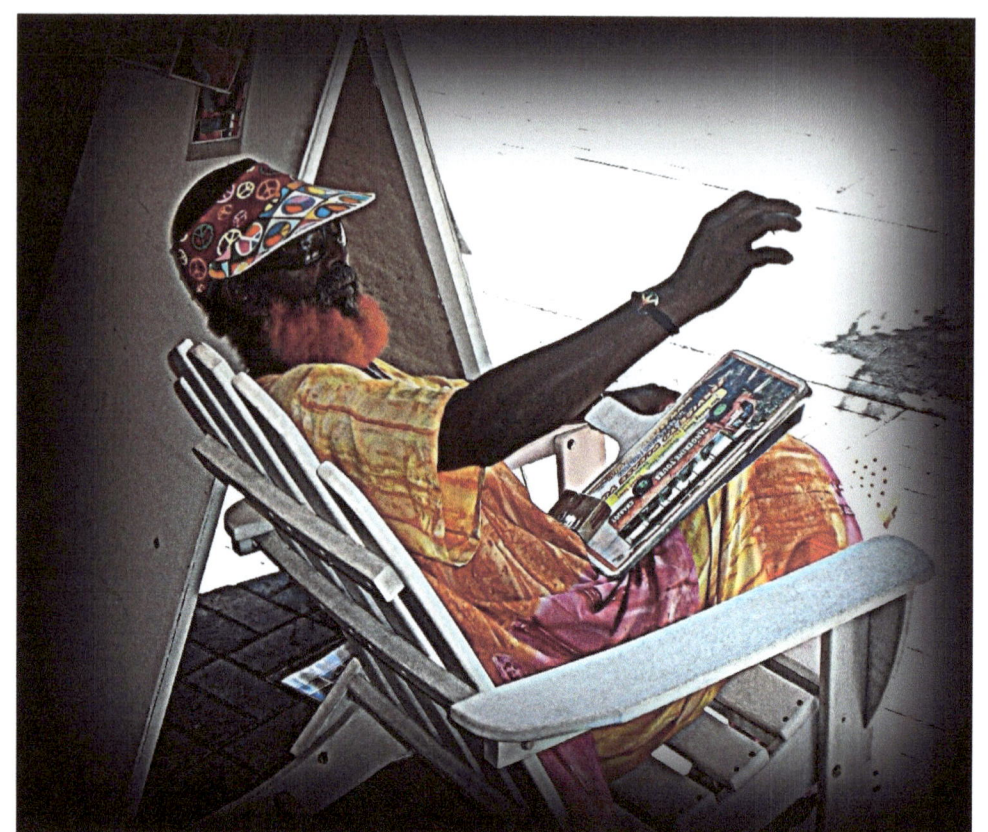

Chillin'

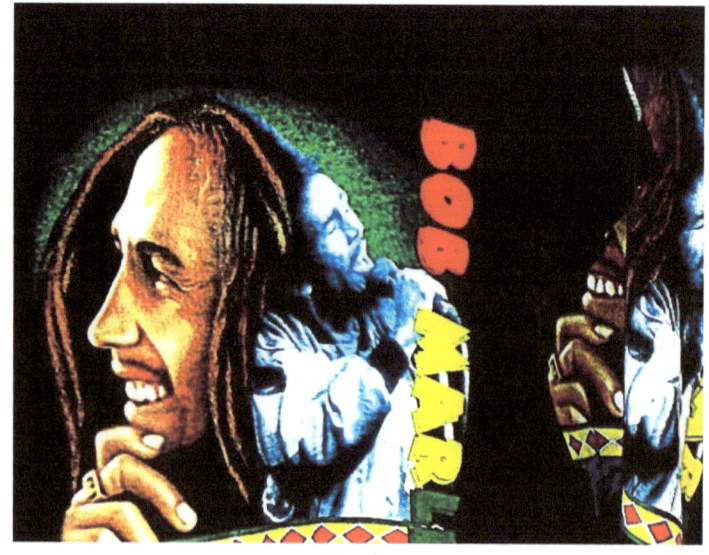

Bob

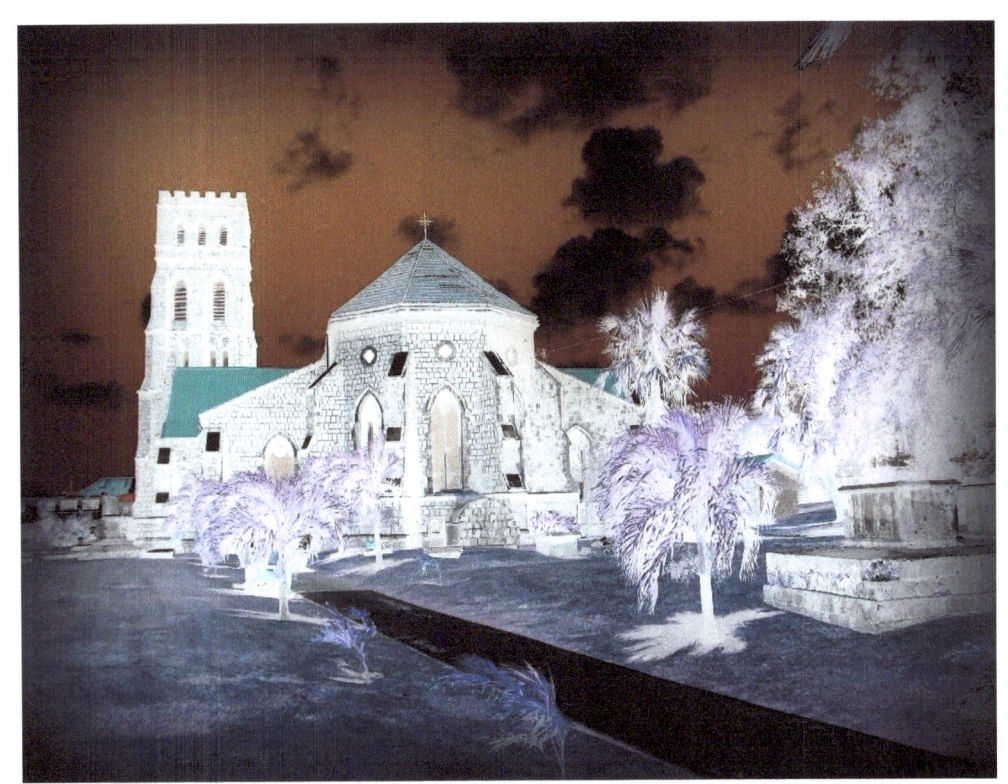

Church Times

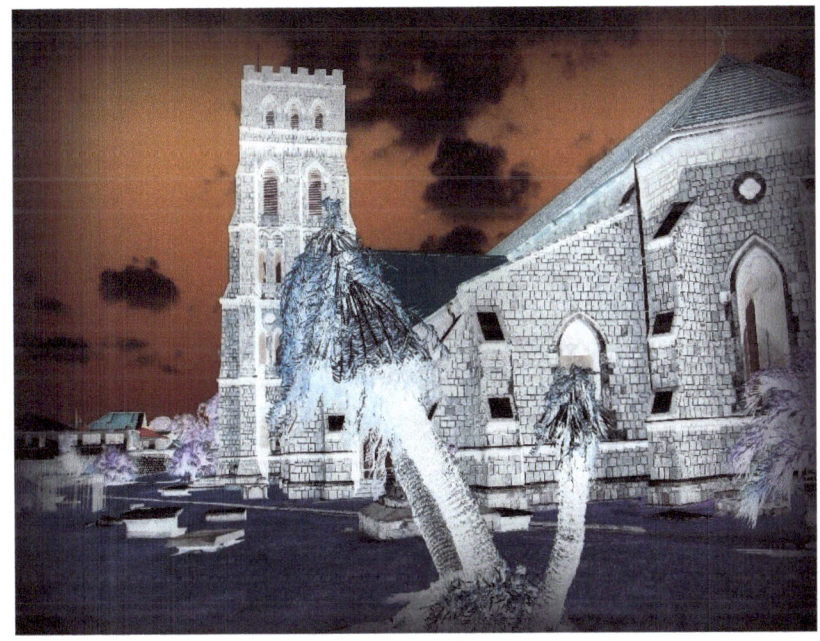

Church Times II

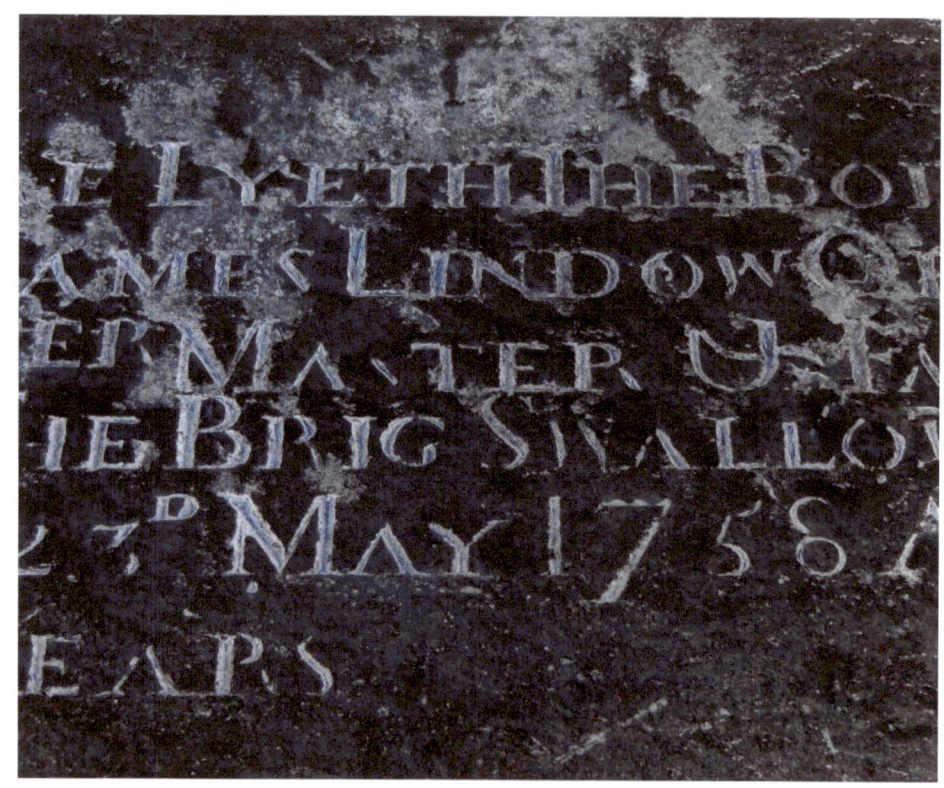

Set in Stone

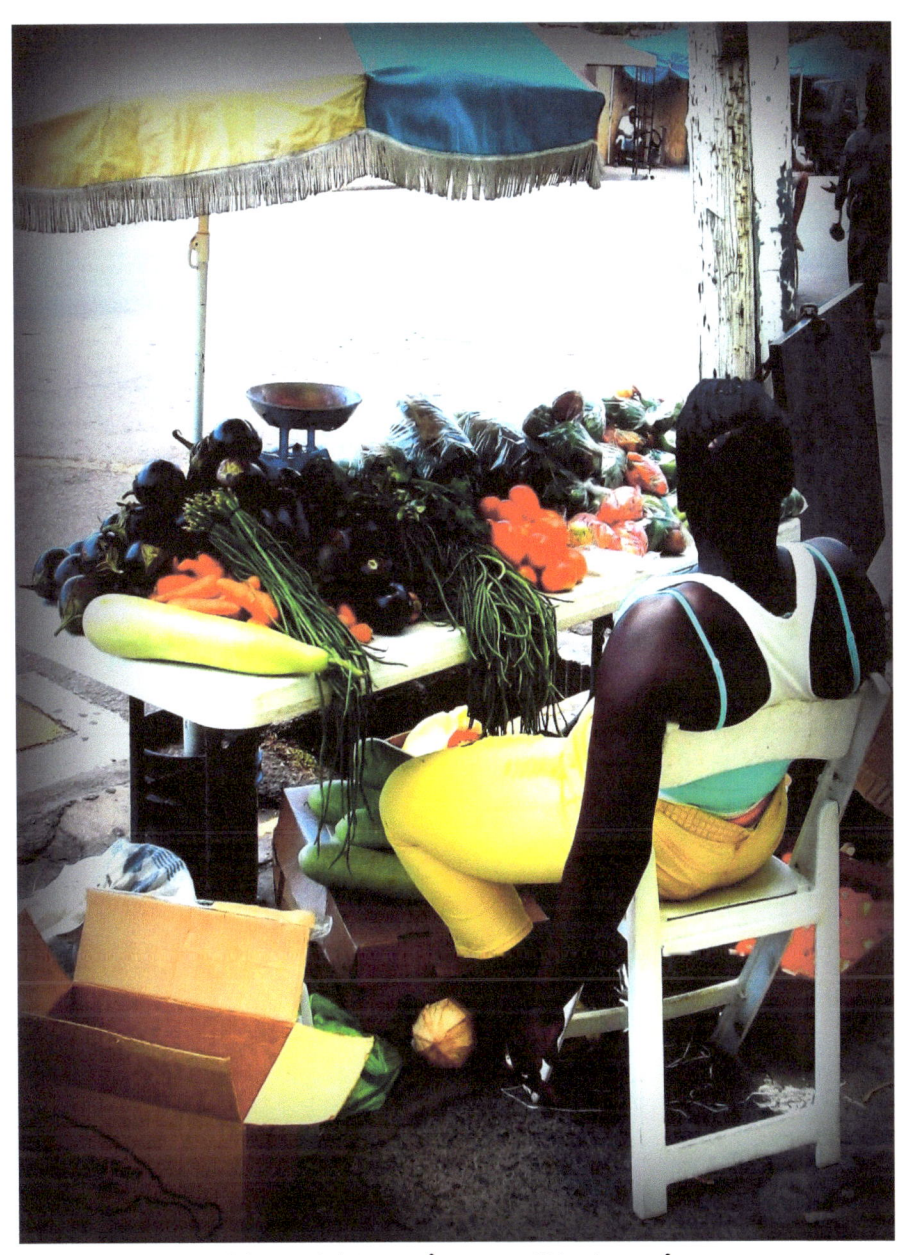

Street Vendor - St. Lucia

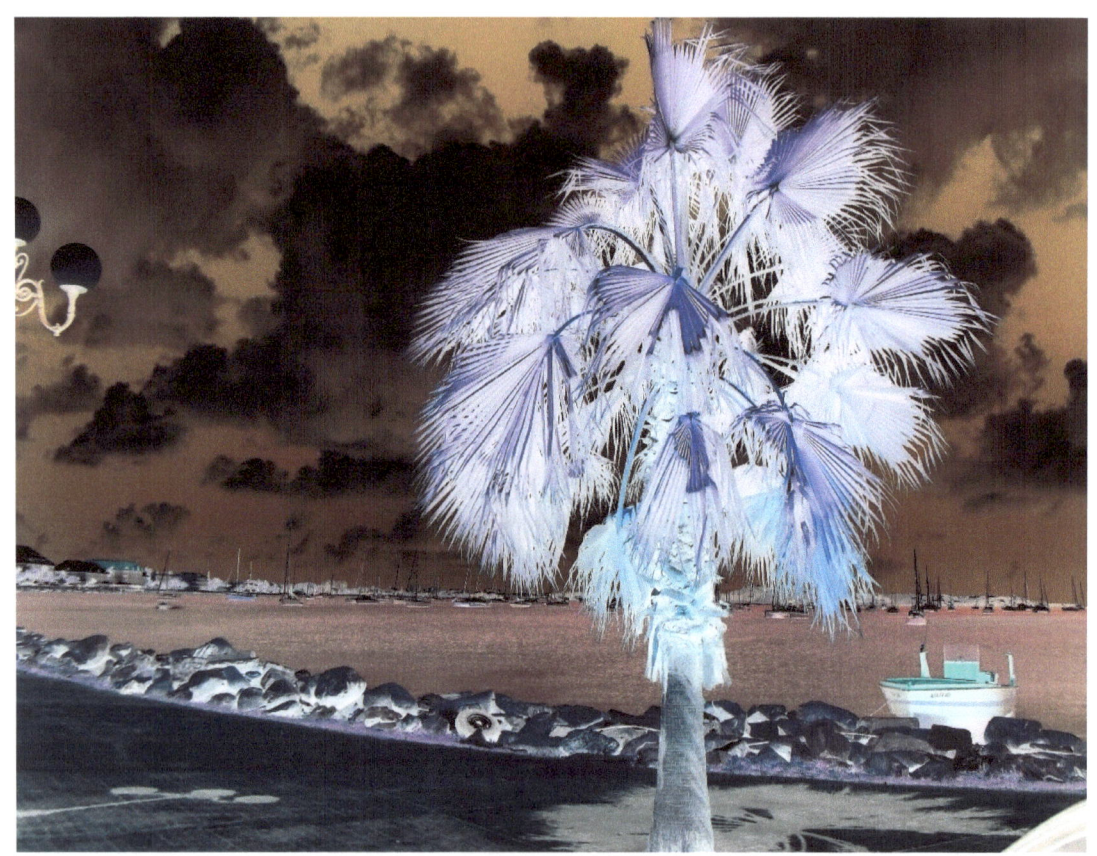

Harbor Lights

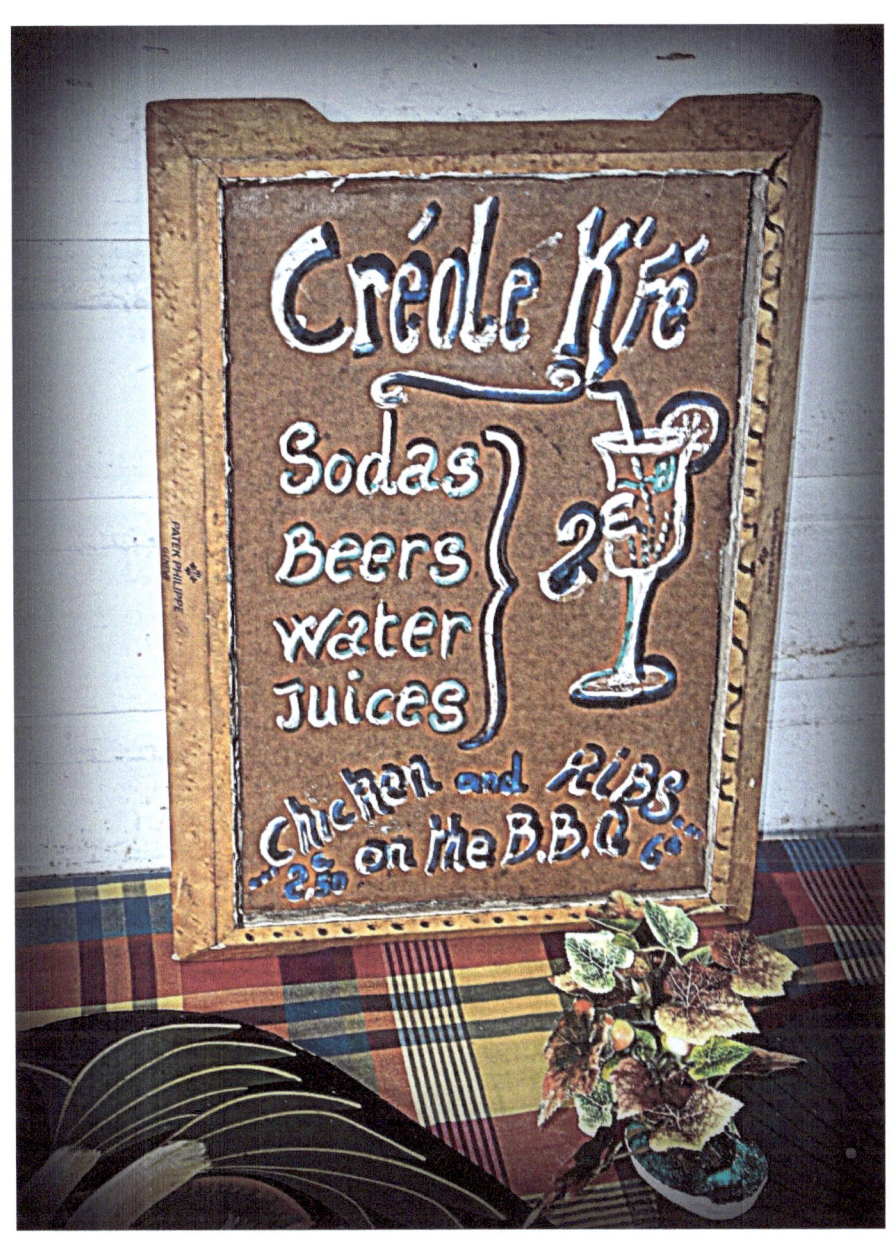

Decisions, Decisions....

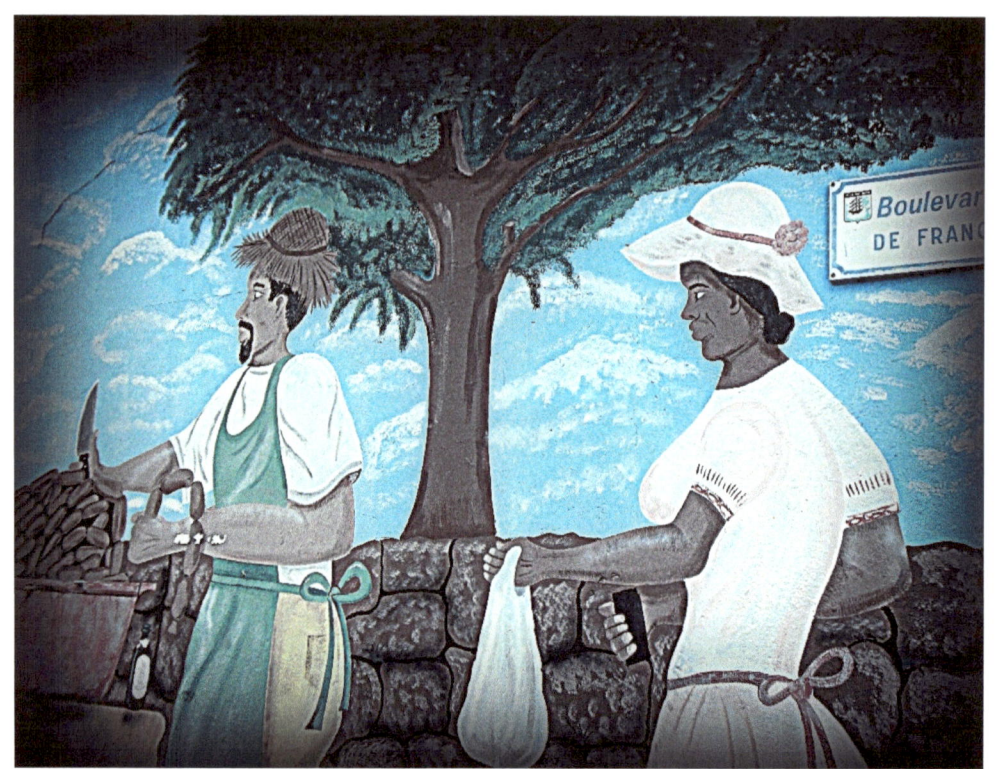

Wall Art

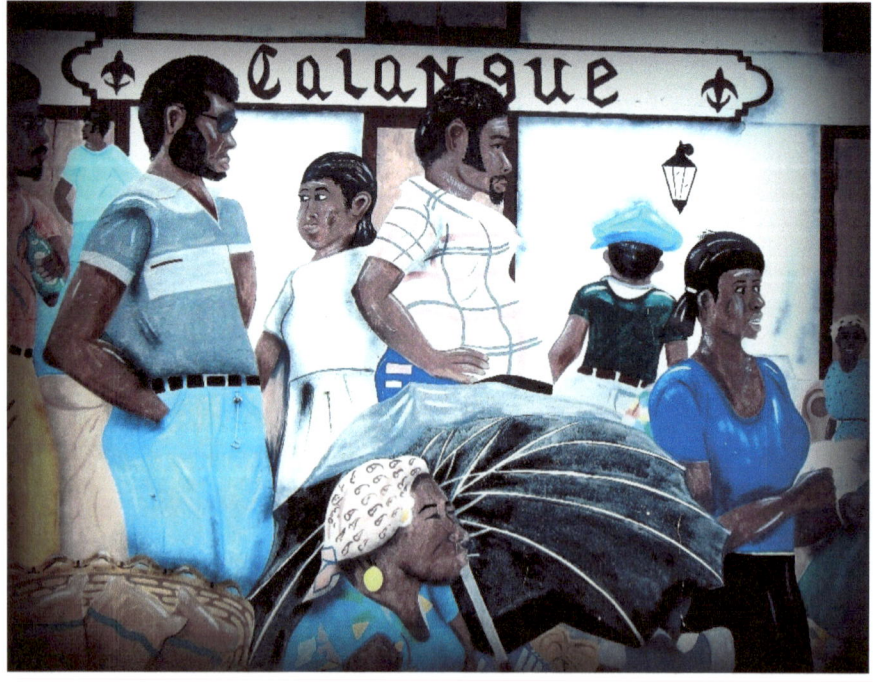

Wall Art II

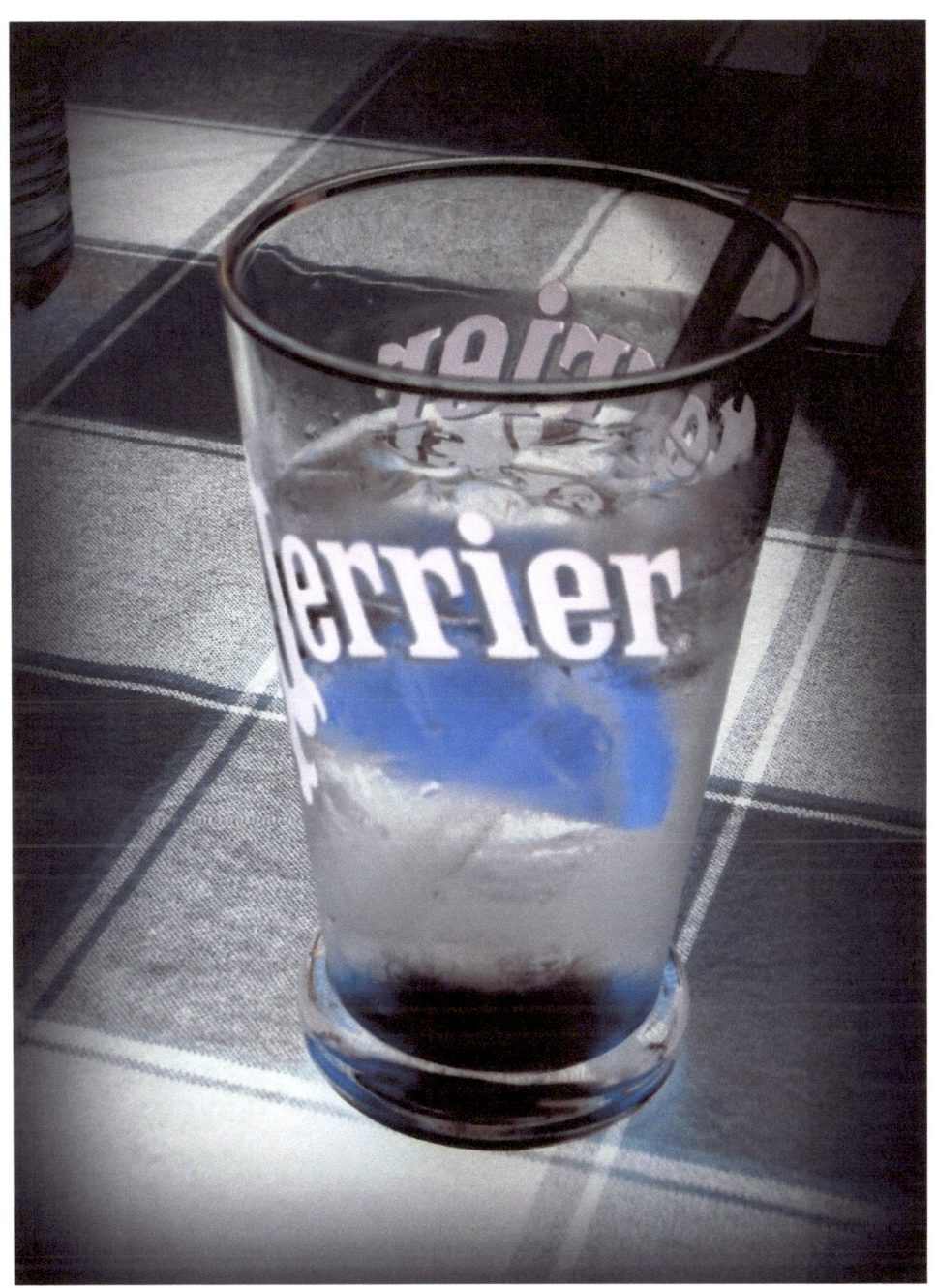

Perrier II

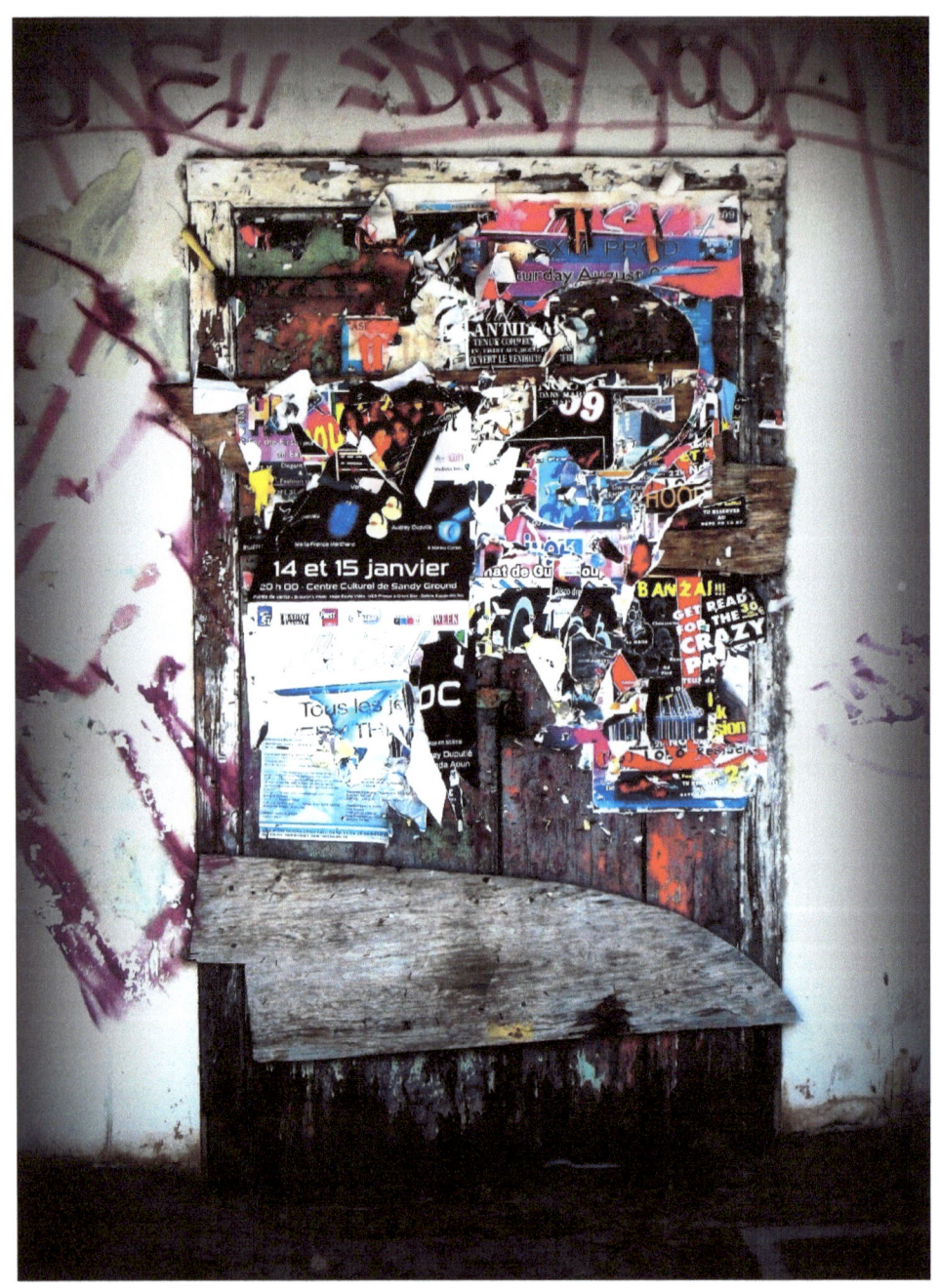

St. Maarten

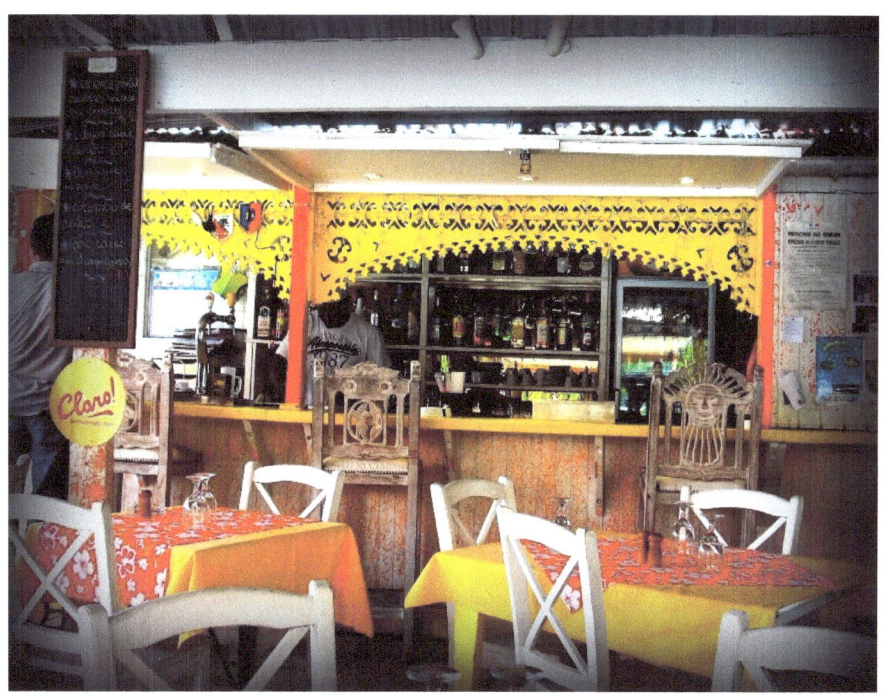

Lunch Time....Again

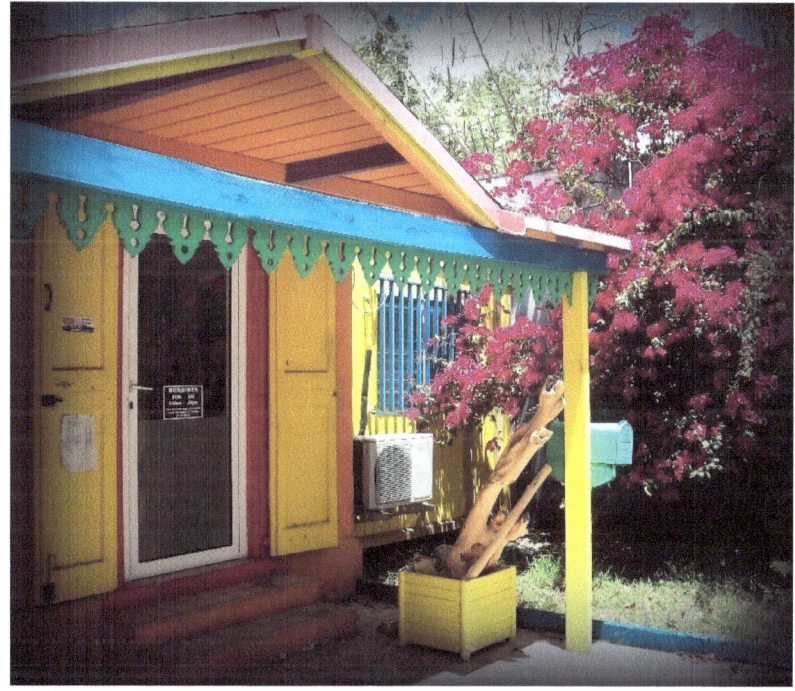

The Doctor is in......

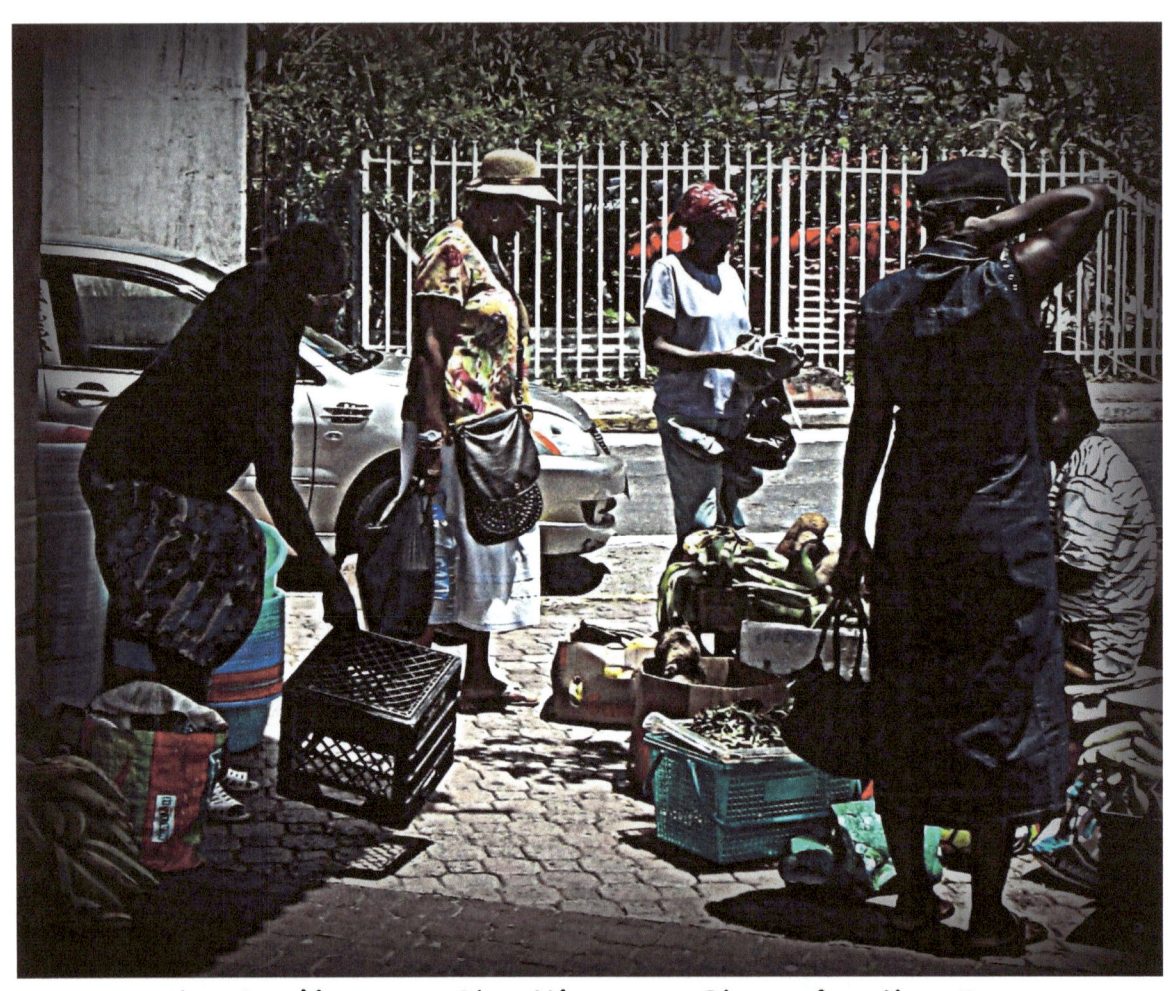

The Ladies are Shutting up Shop for the Day

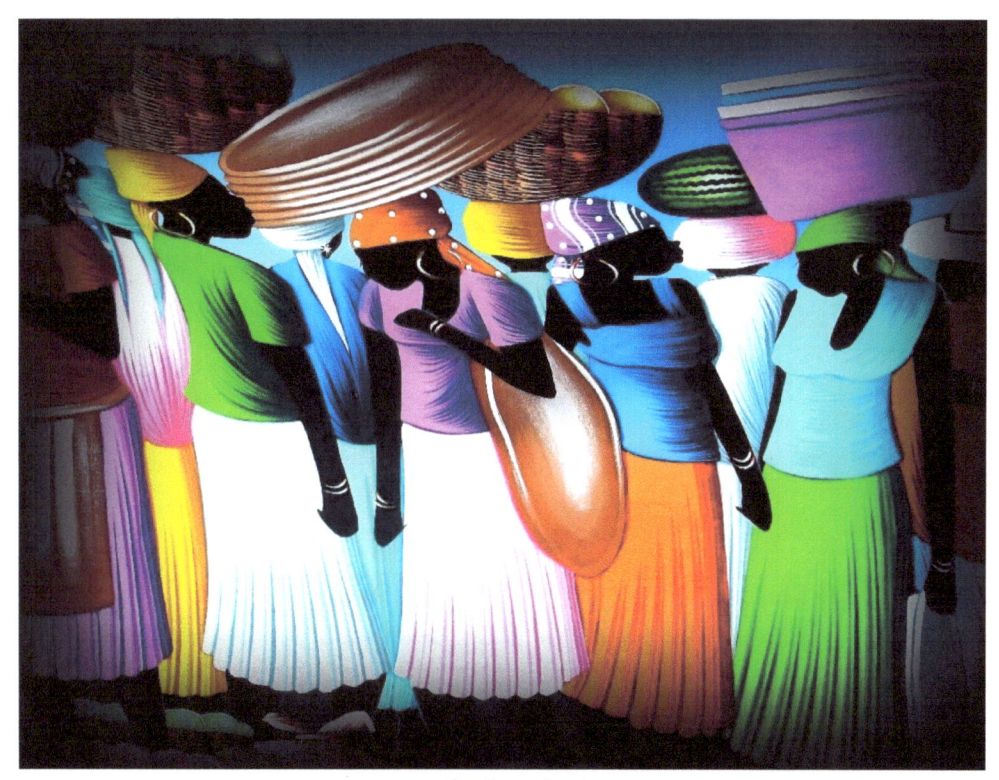

Wall Art

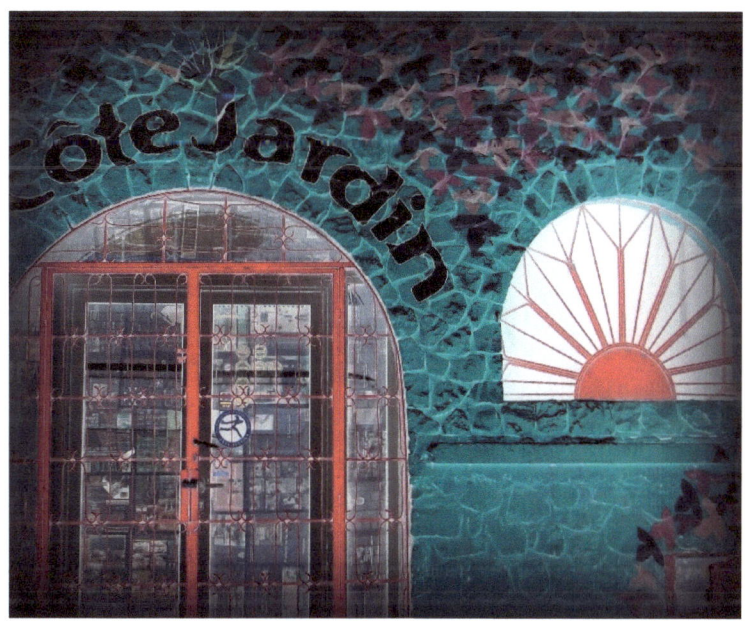

Cote Jardin

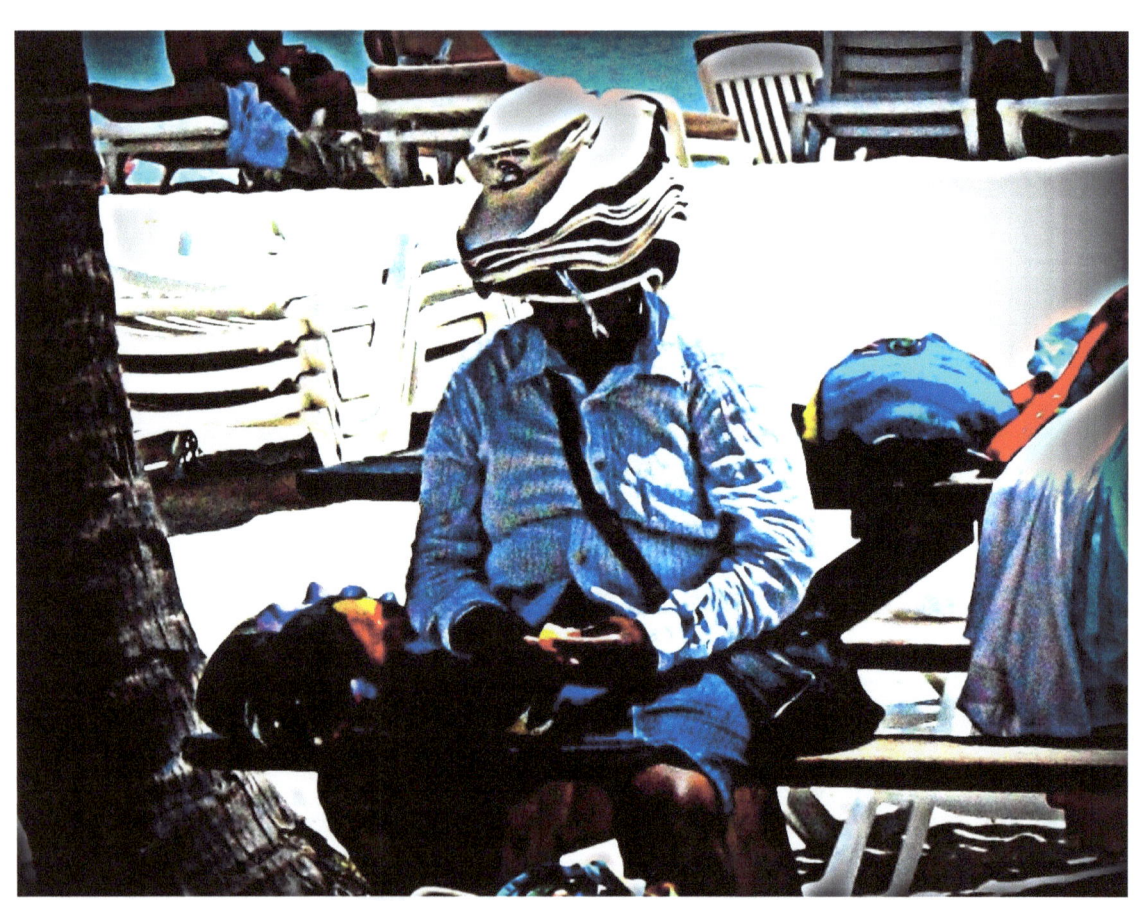

Hat vendor in the Sun

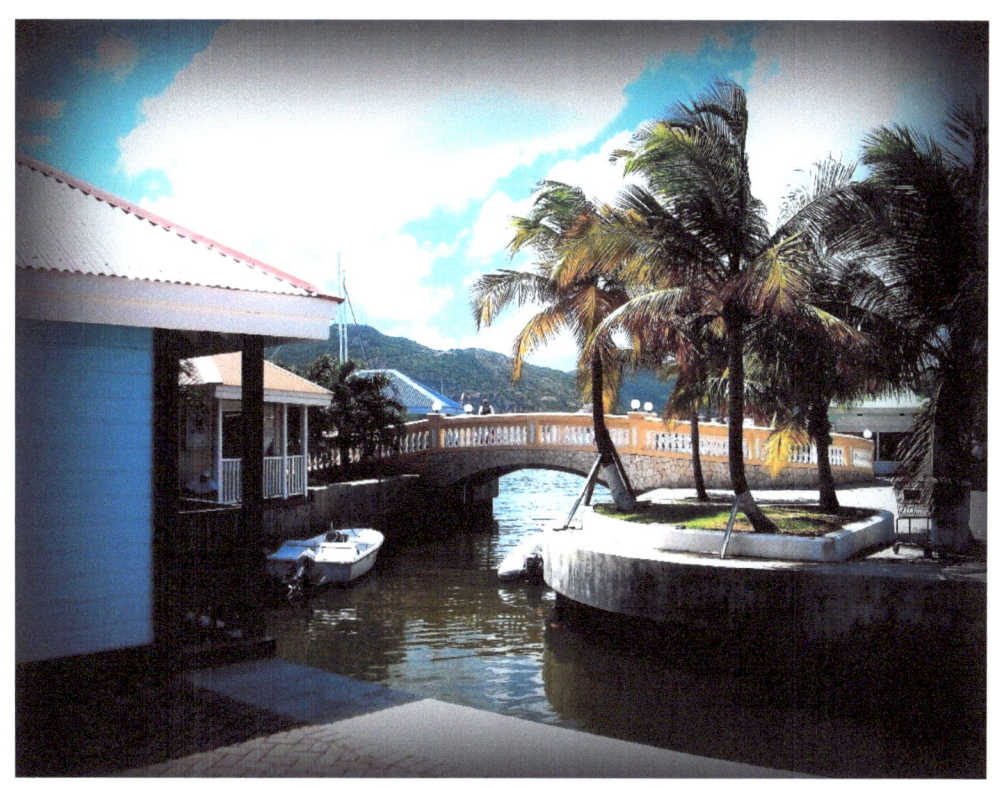

Not the Bridge of Sighs

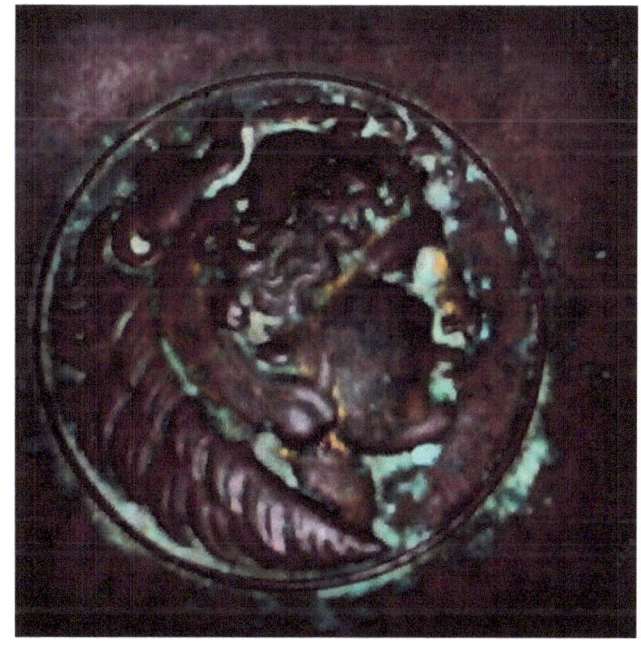

Alexander the Great

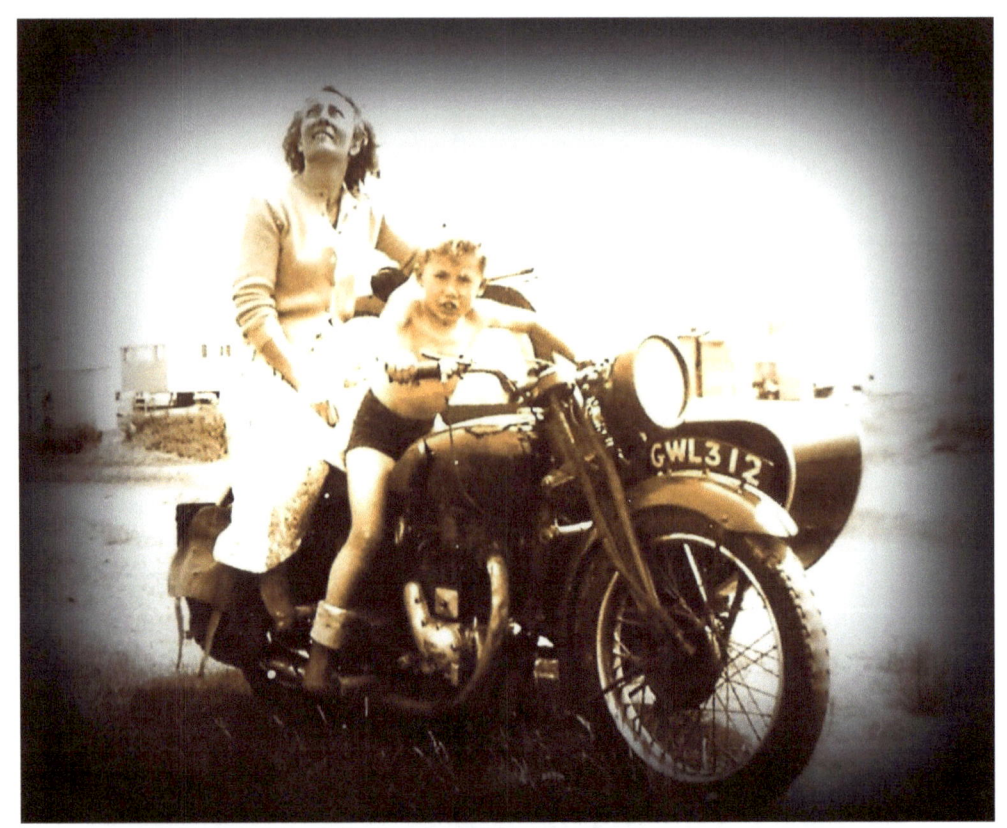

Happy Days

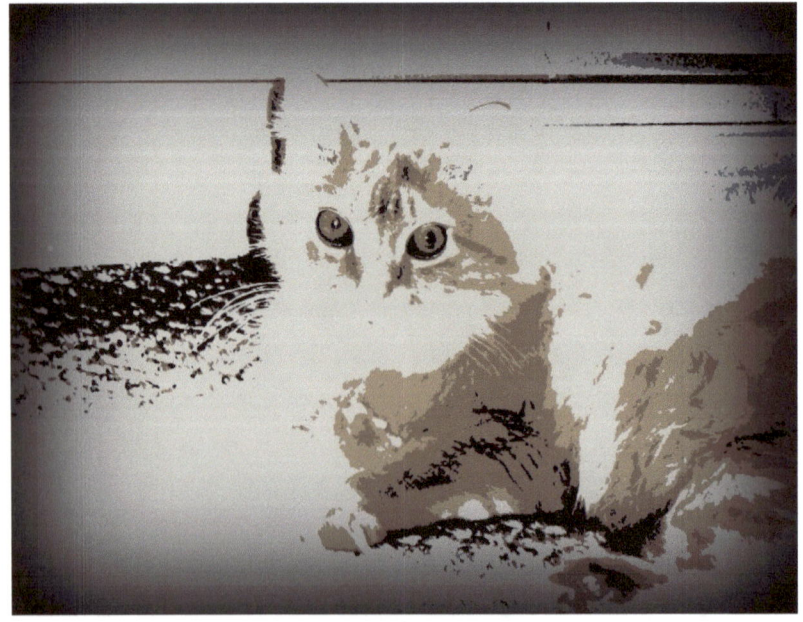

The Muppet

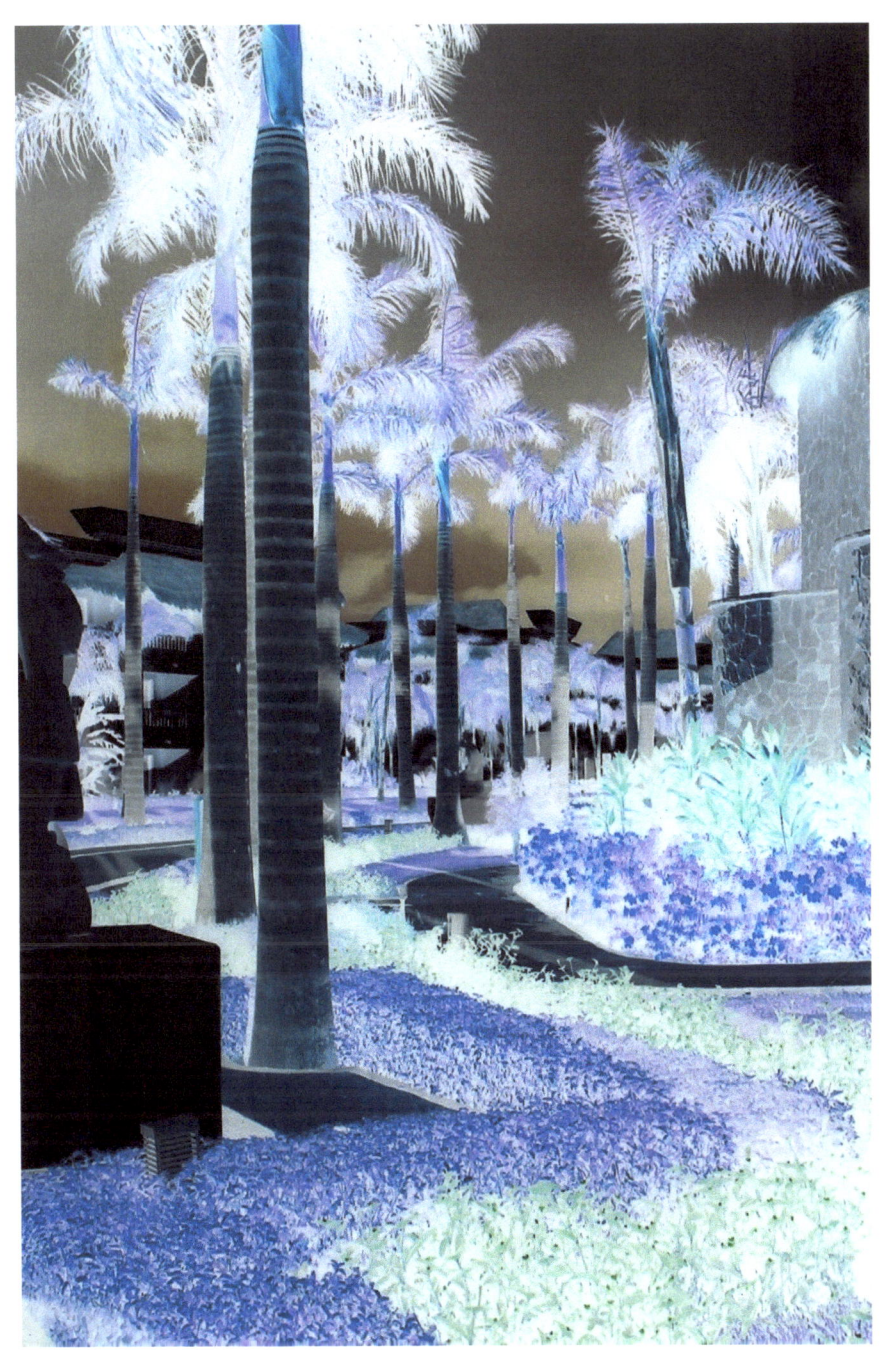

Purple Haze

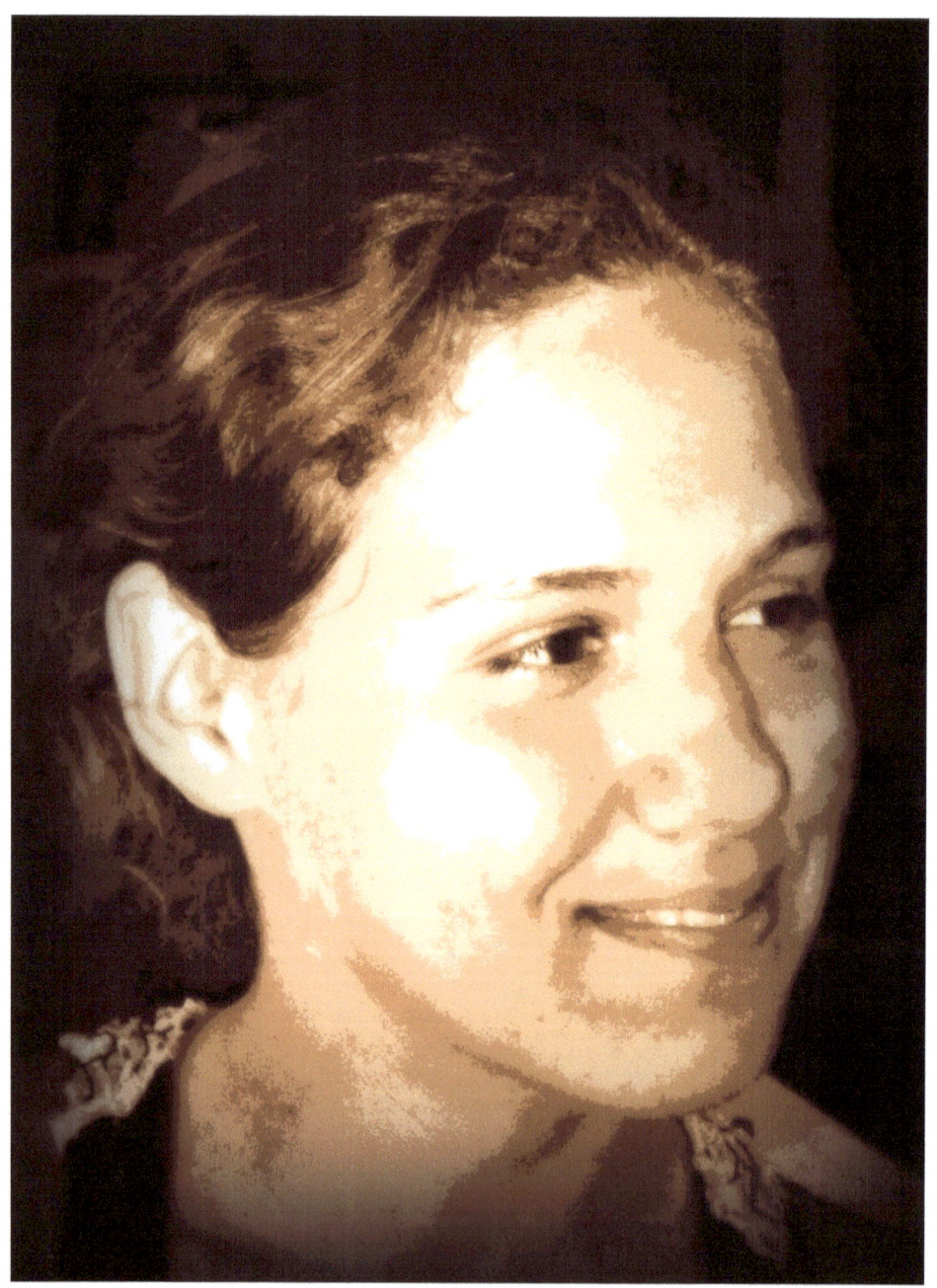

Lydia

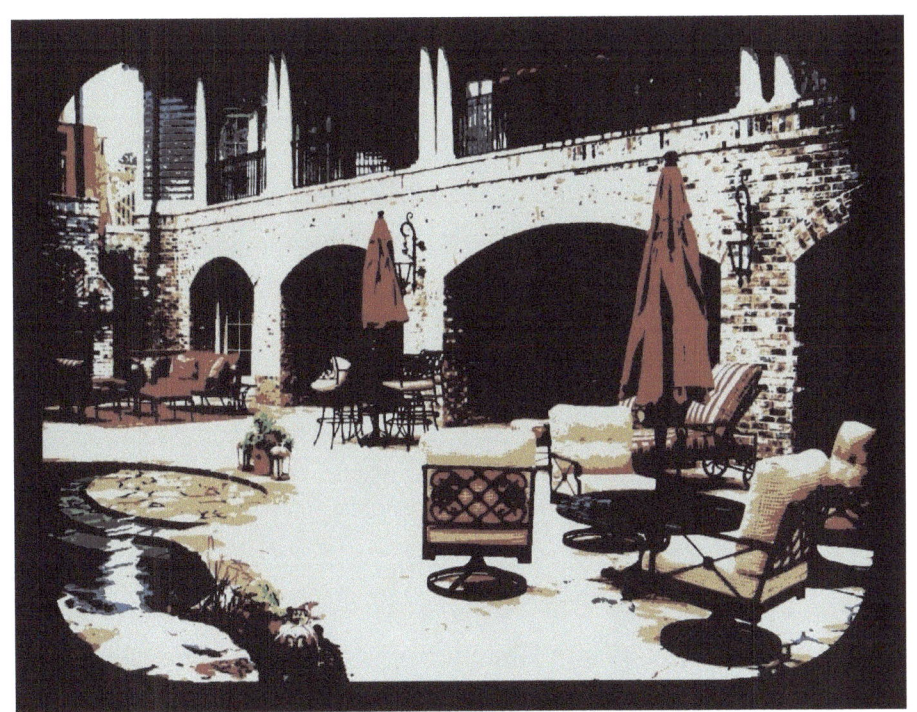

House in Georgia

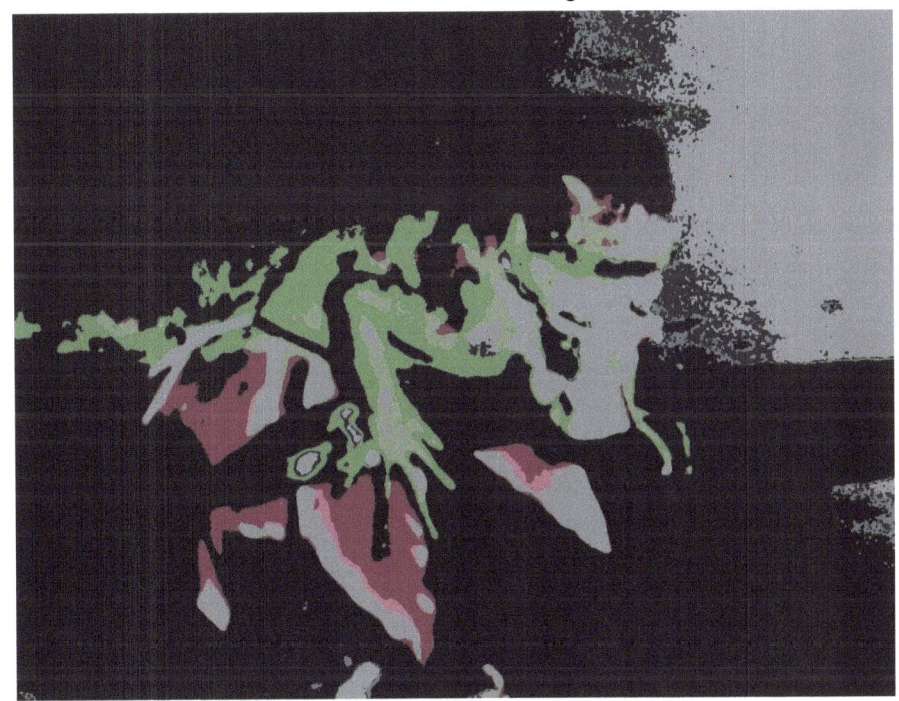

Cool Critter

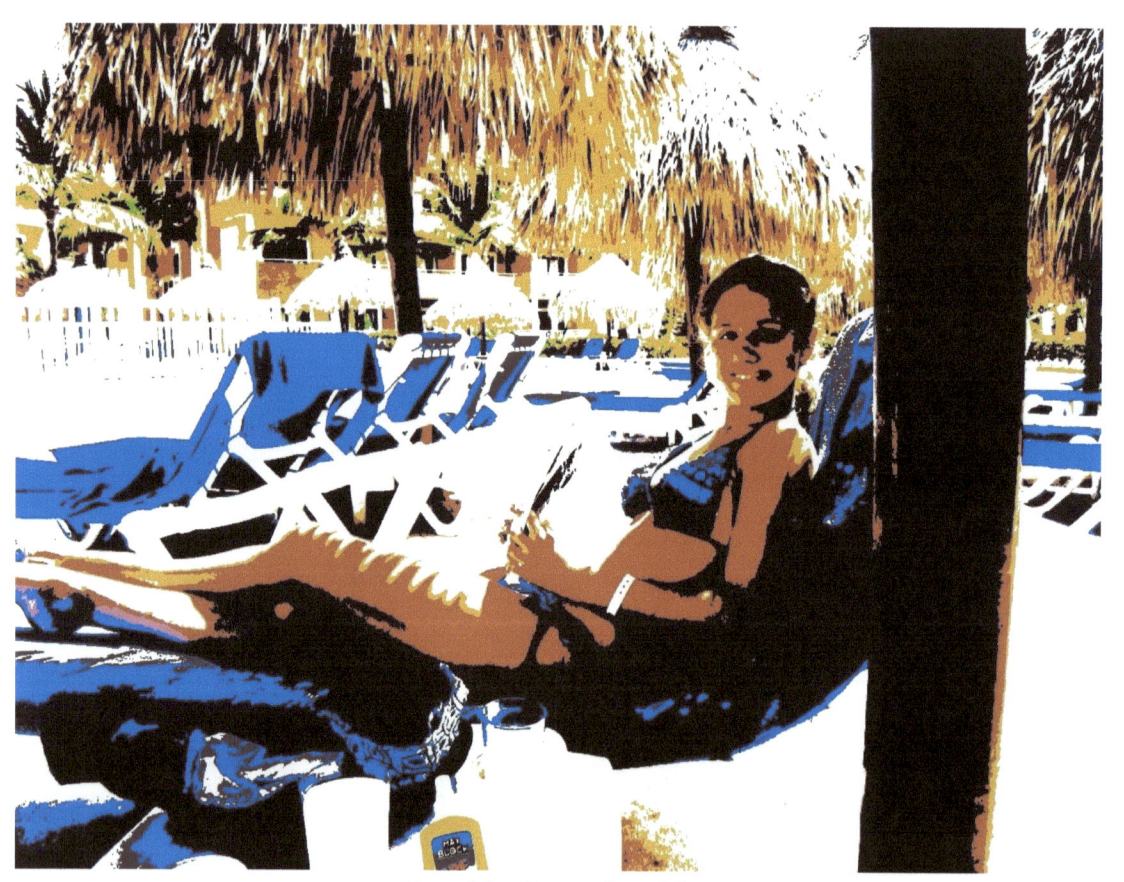

Reclining Lydia

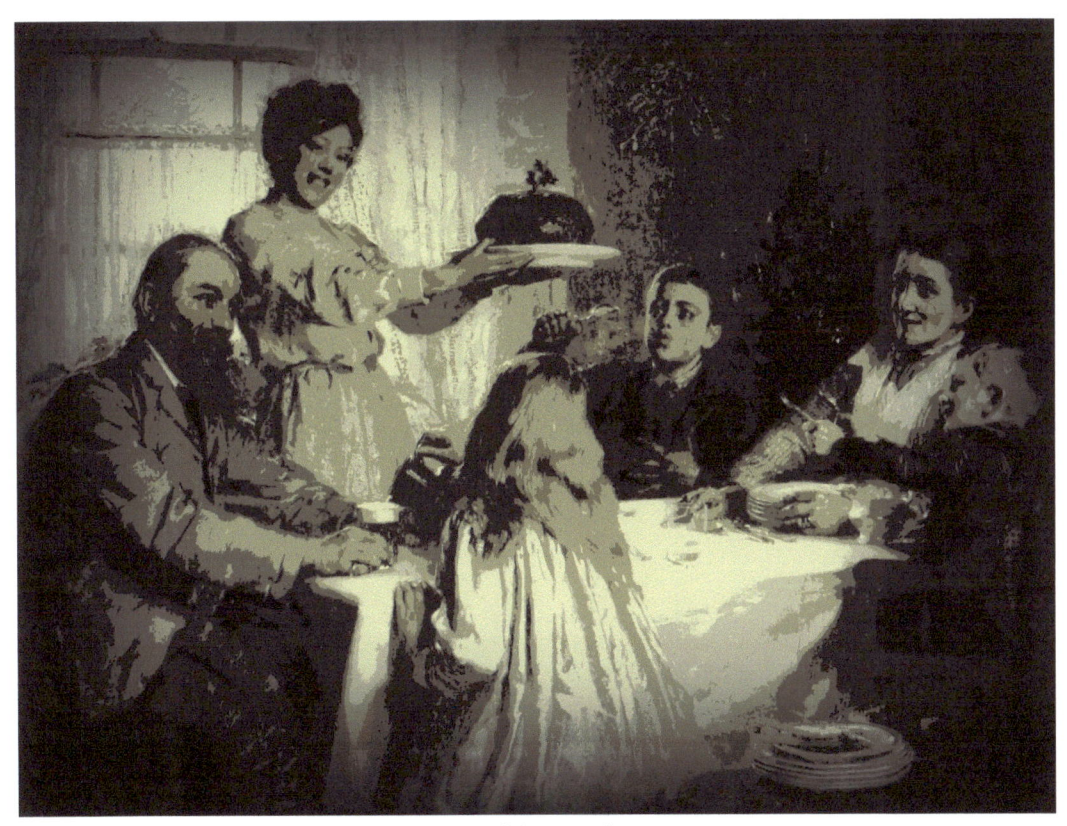

A Family Dinner

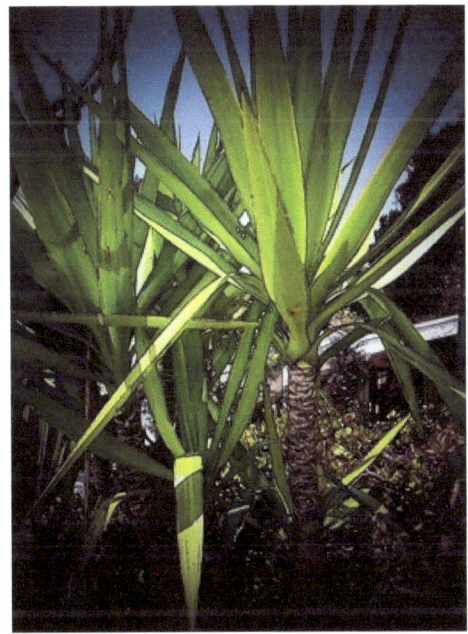

A Little Vegetation

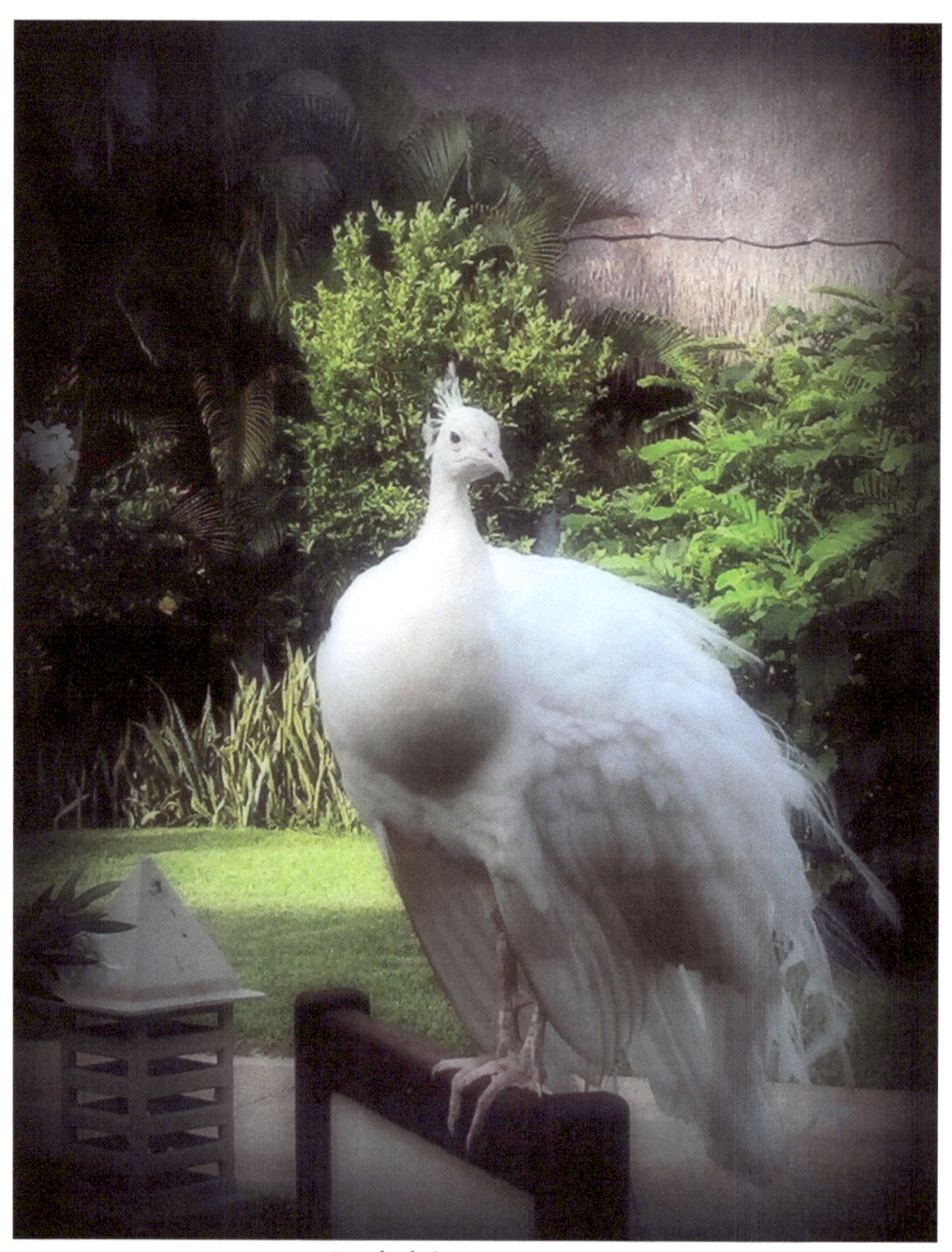

A Noble Creature

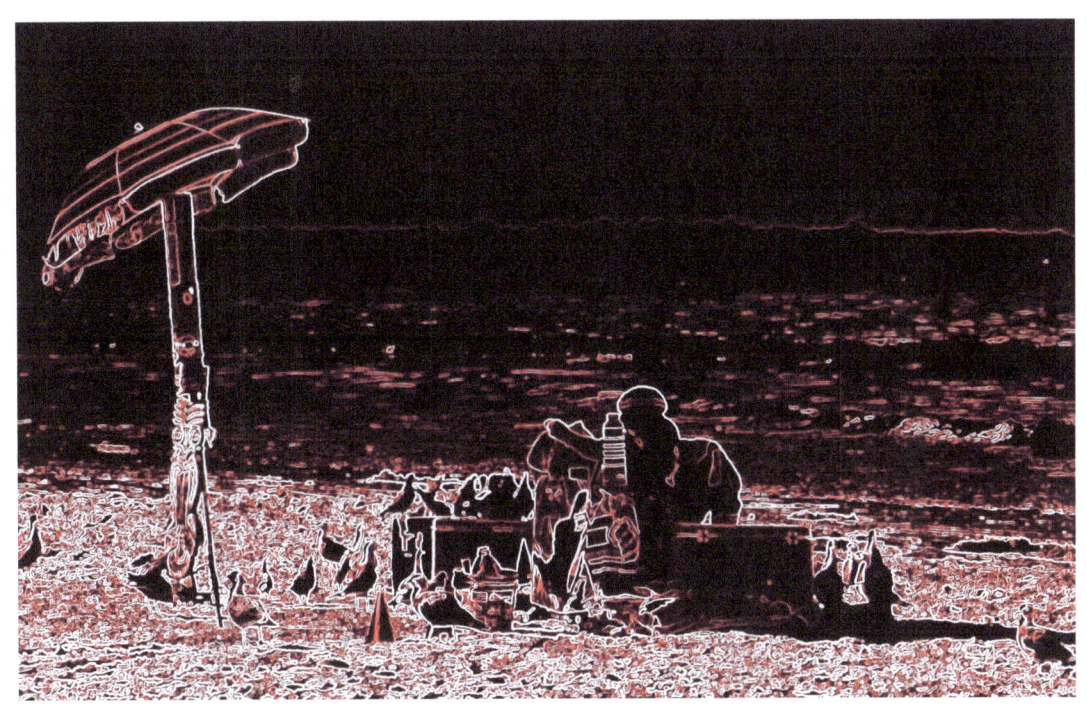

A Beach Bum

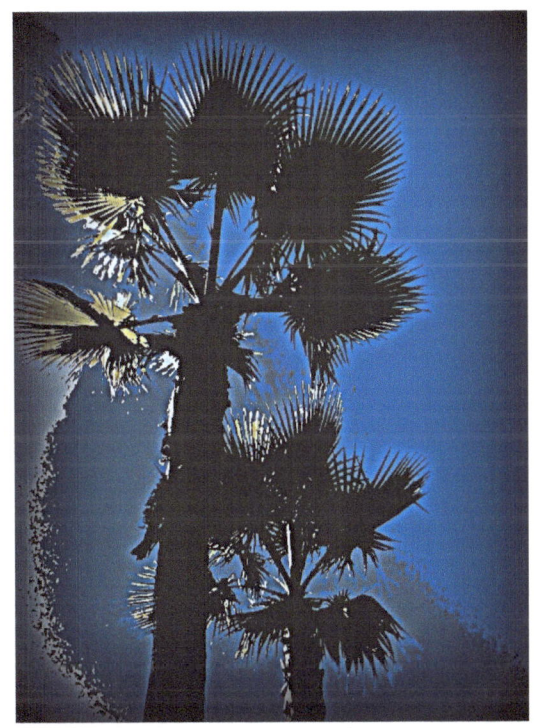

Branch Office

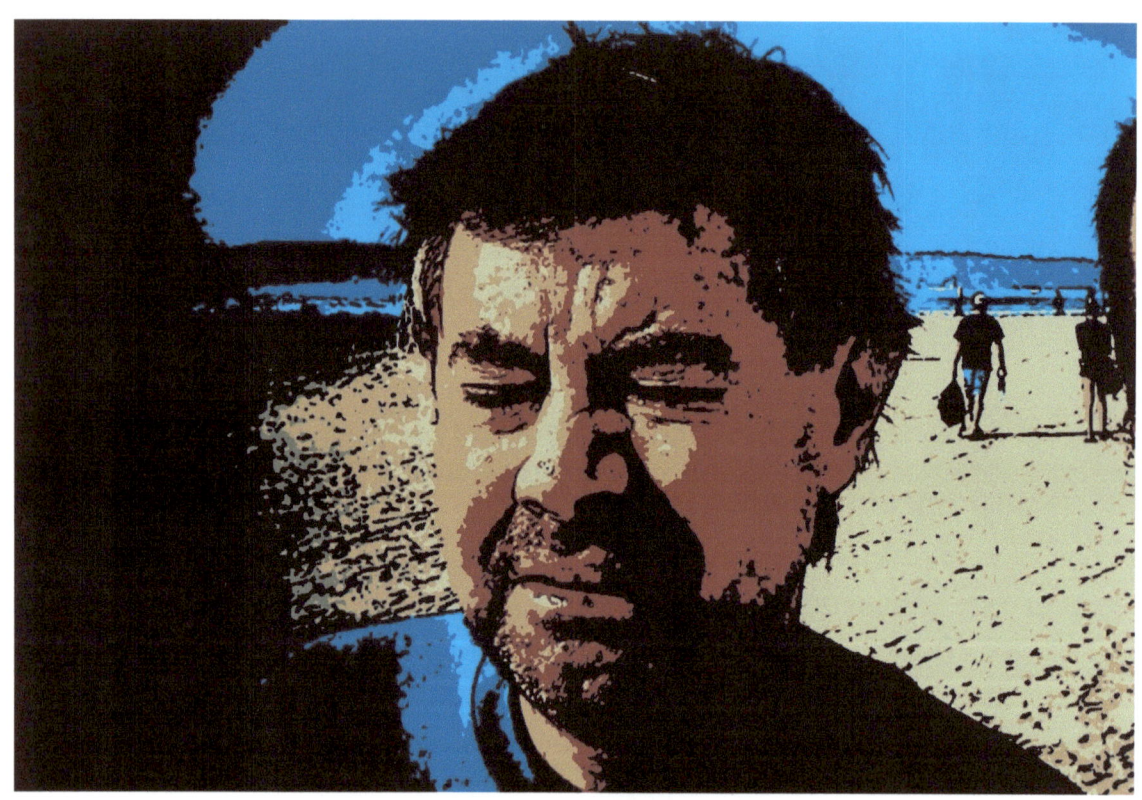

Pensive Paul

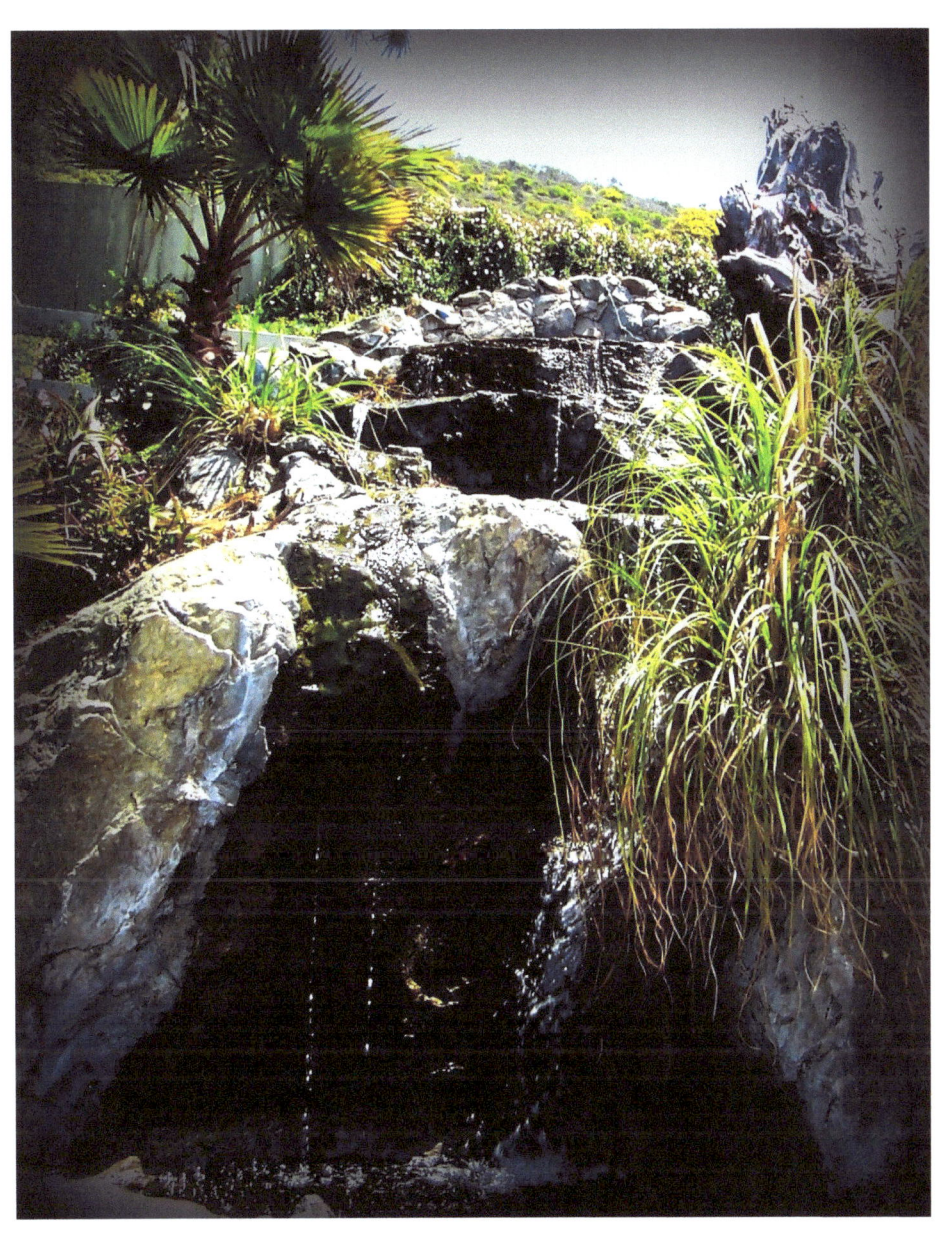

California Dreaming

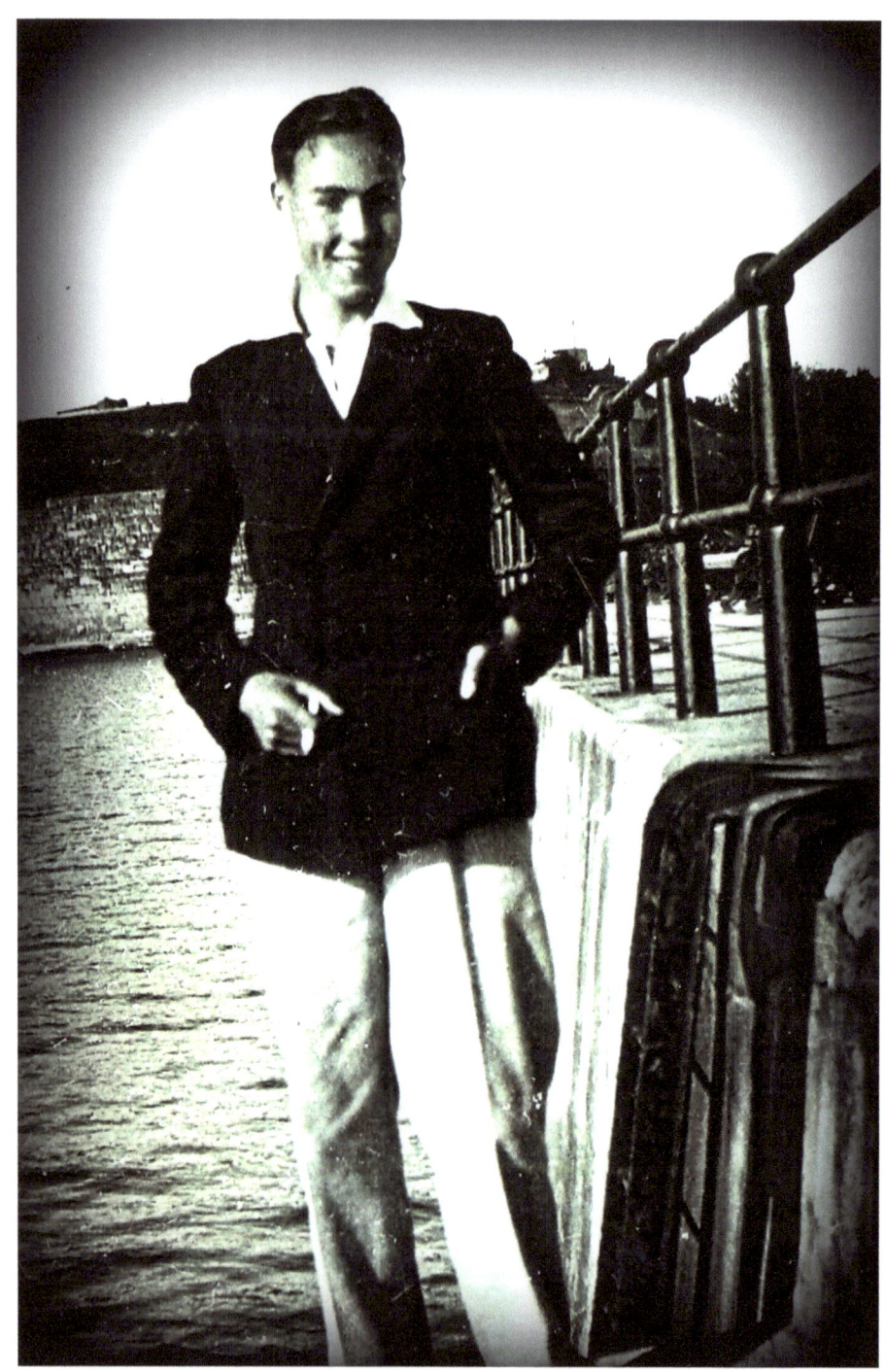

The Famous Mr. Pepperell in Weymouth

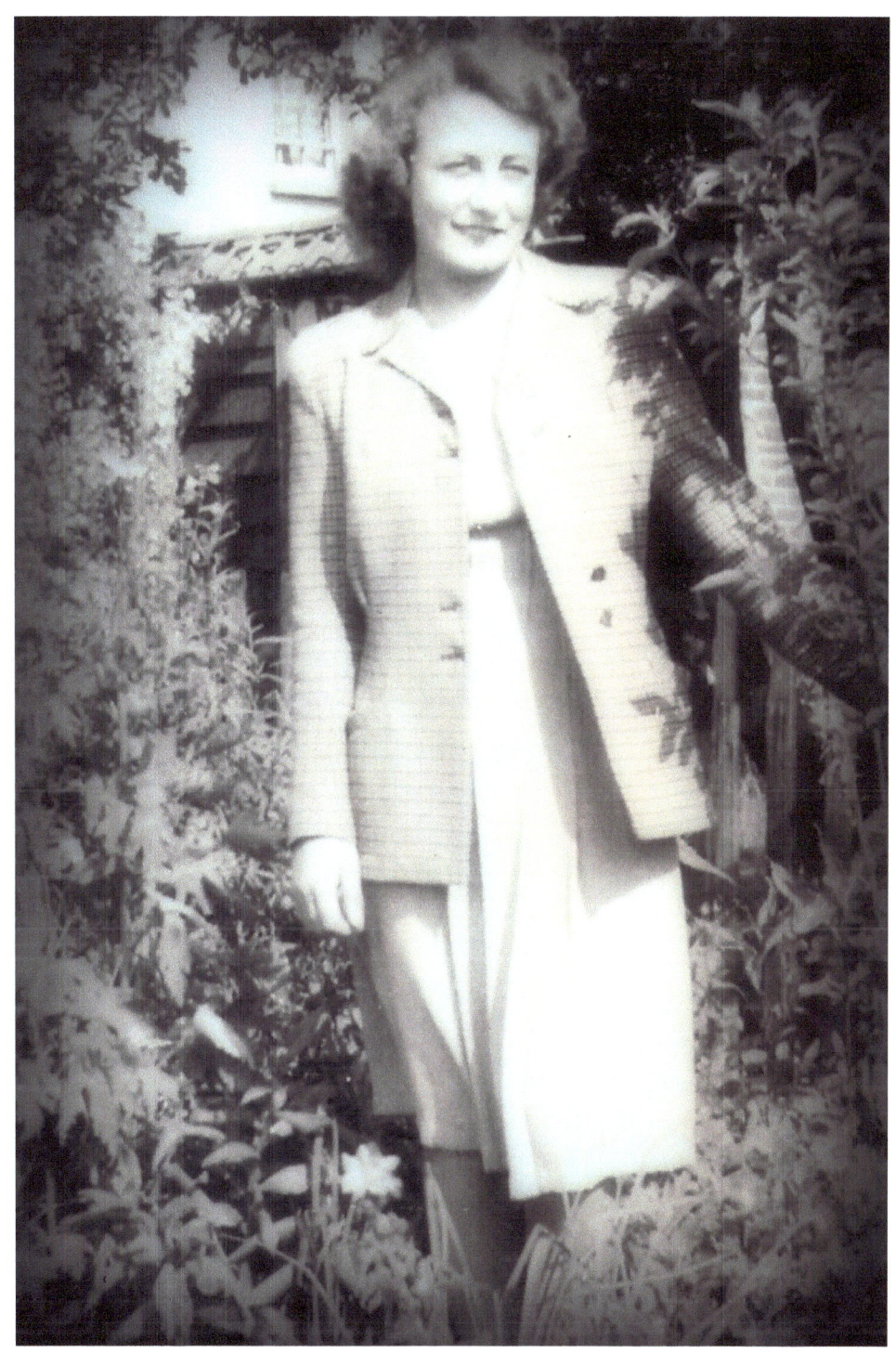

The Famous Lady Joan in Chelmsford

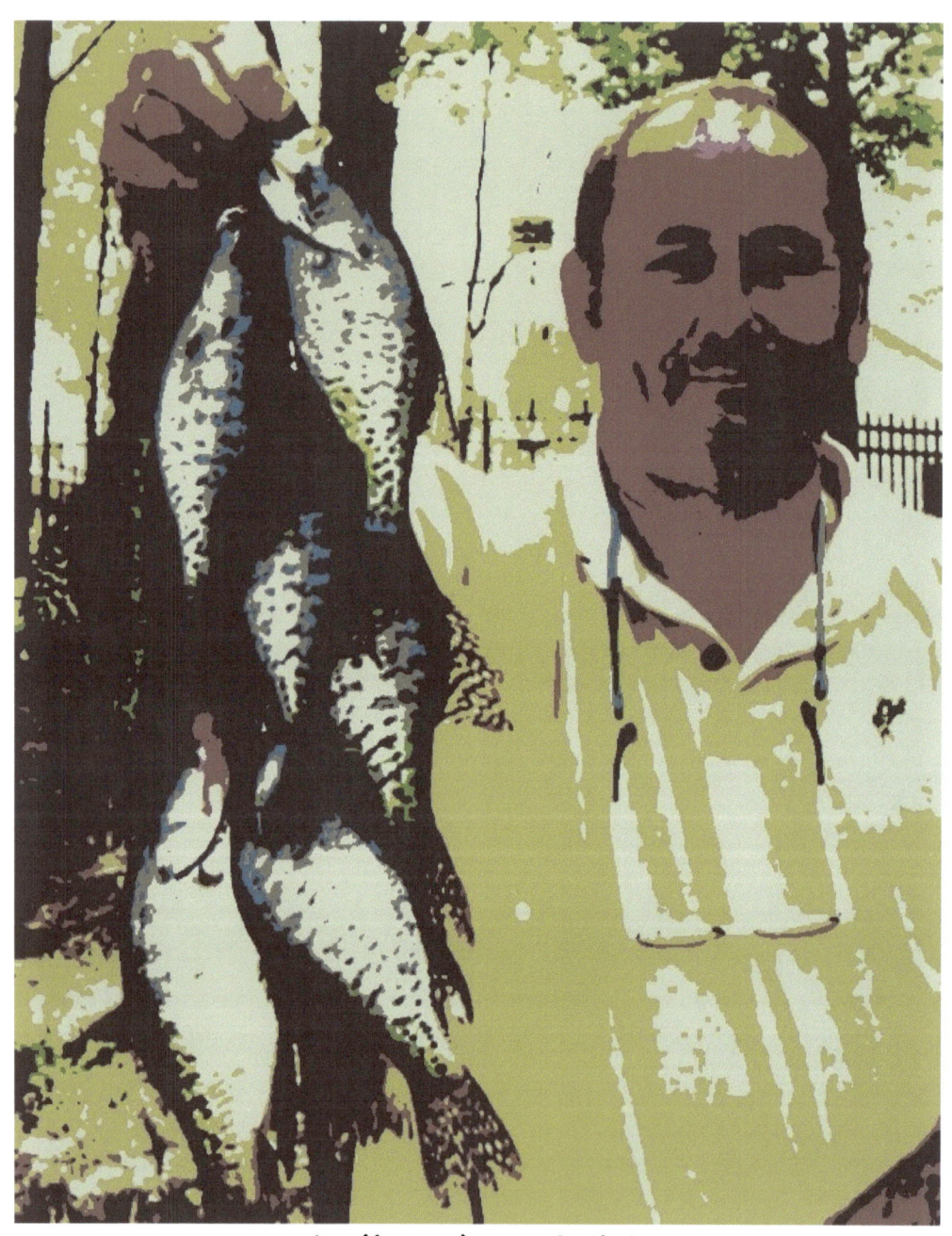

A Nice Mess of Fish

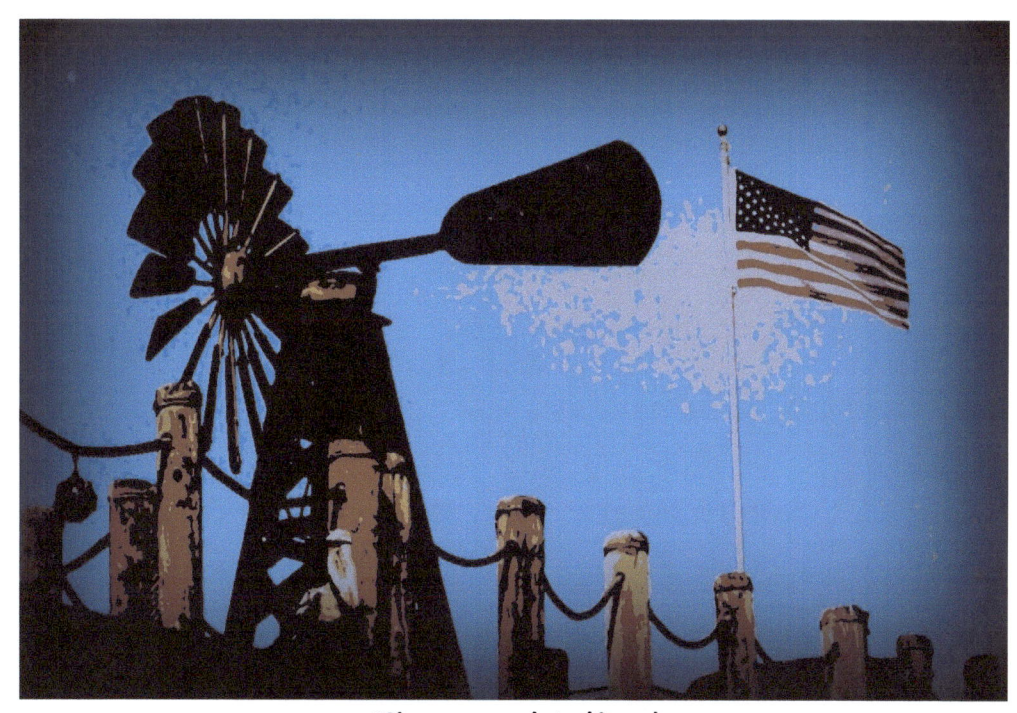

Flag and Wind

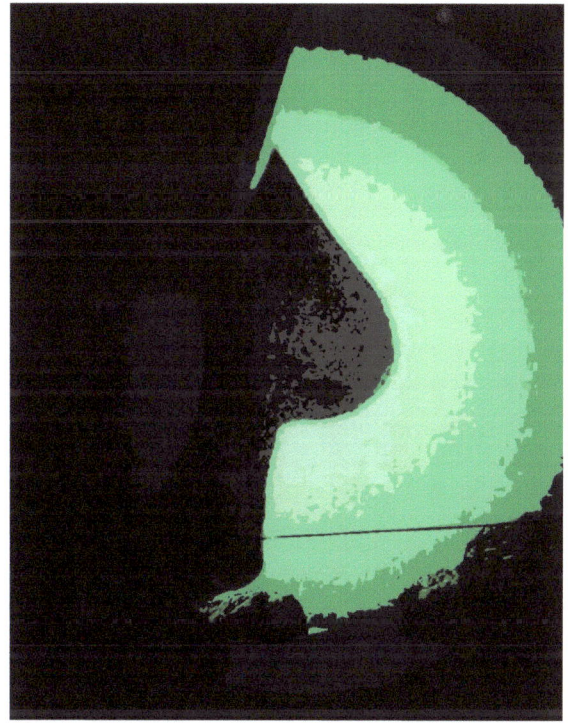

Smelling the Territory

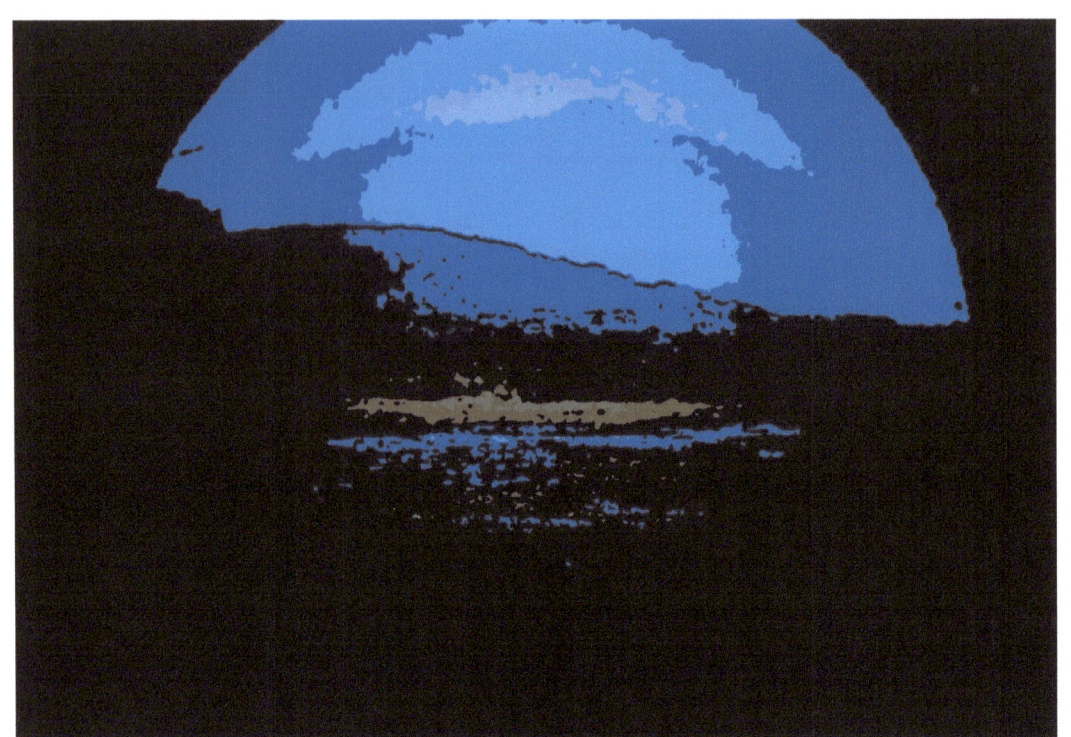

California Morning

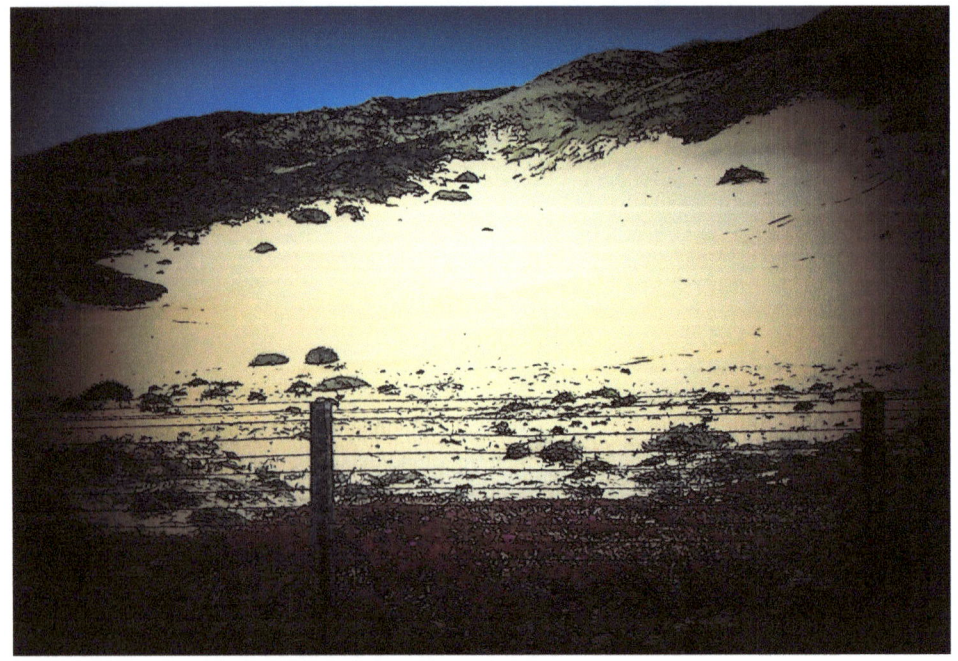

California Road Trip

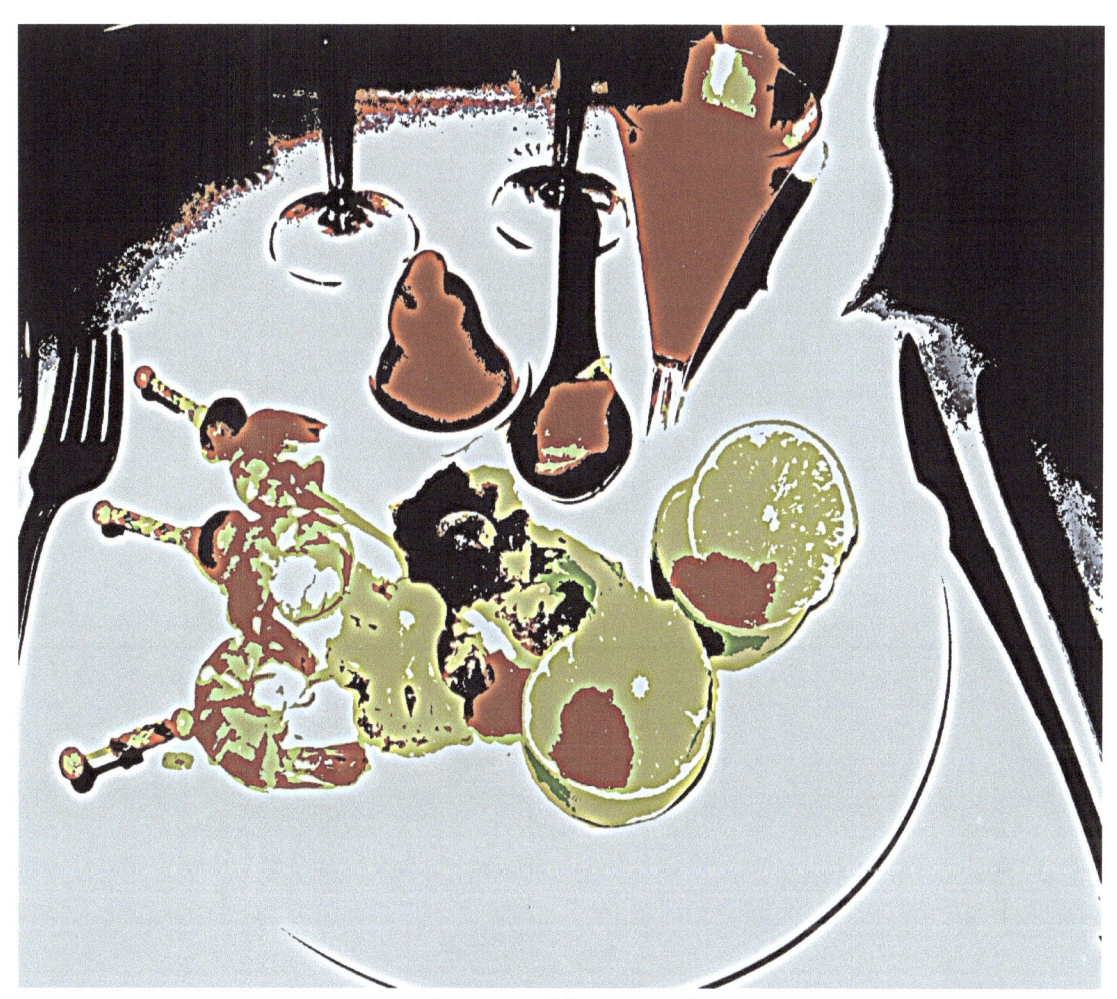

A Small Snack

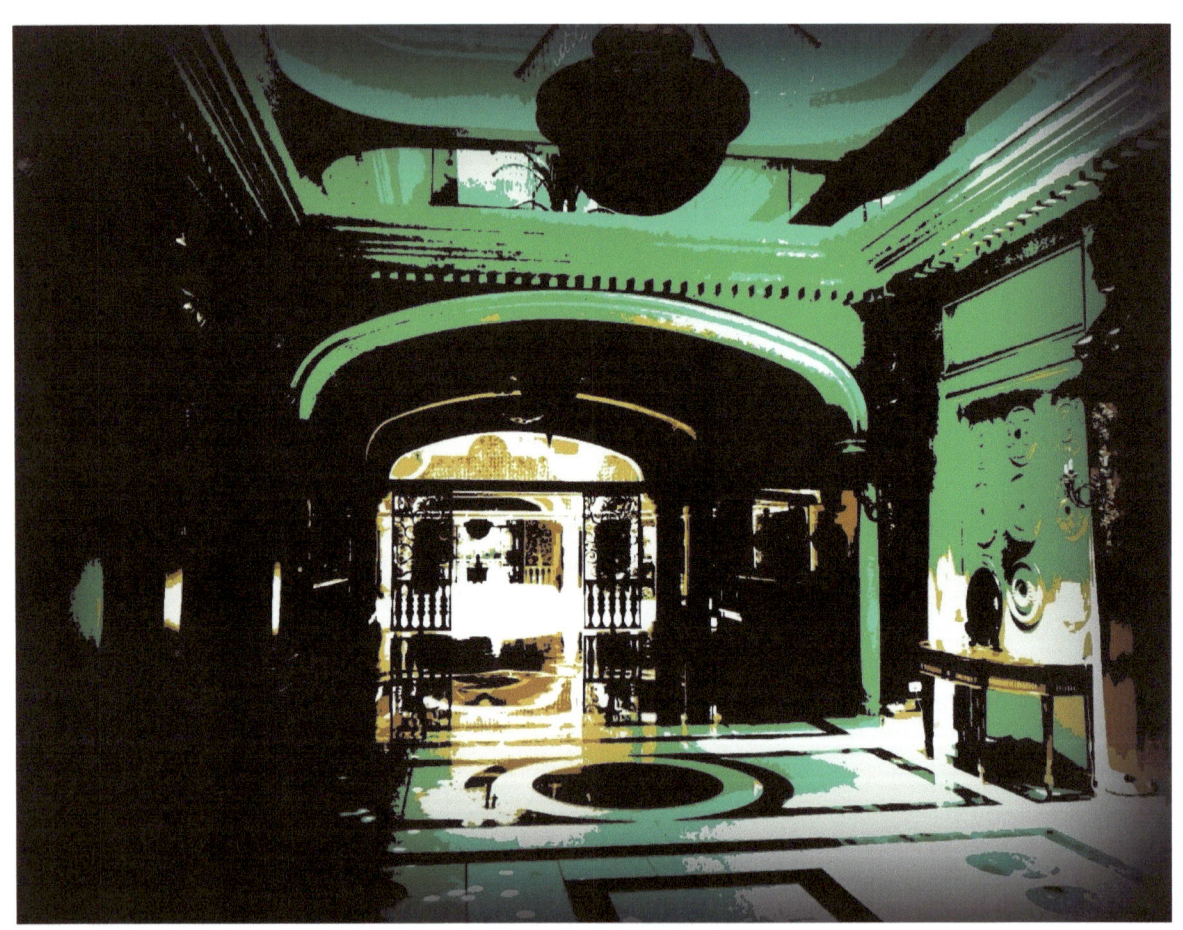

The Lobby

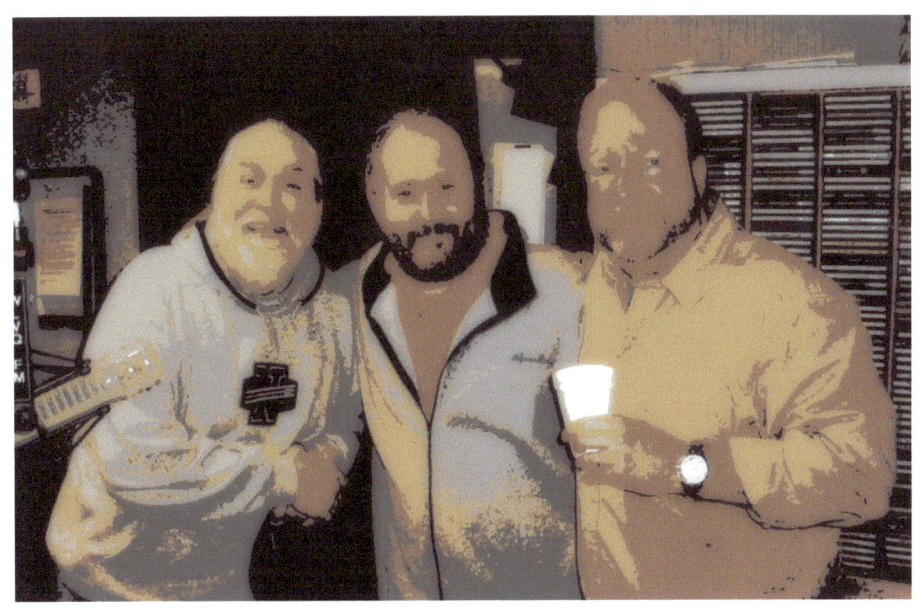

QFM 96 Superstars

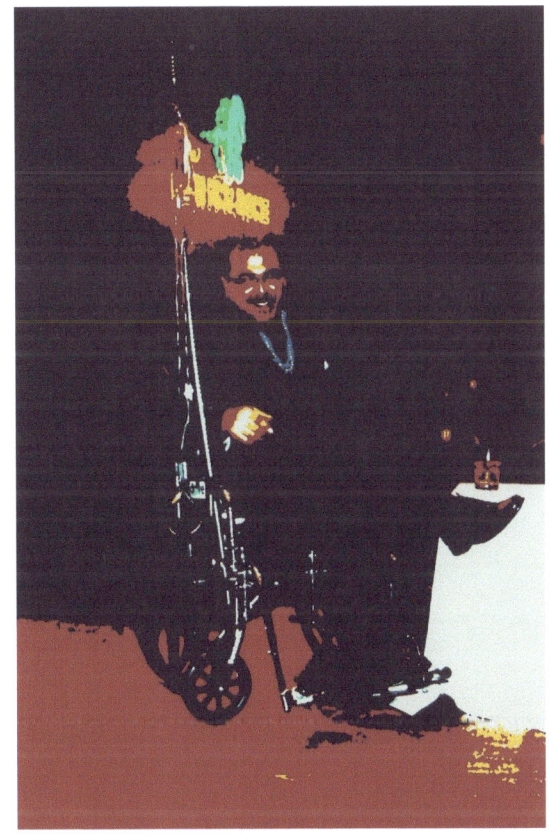

Dino Tripodis Roast

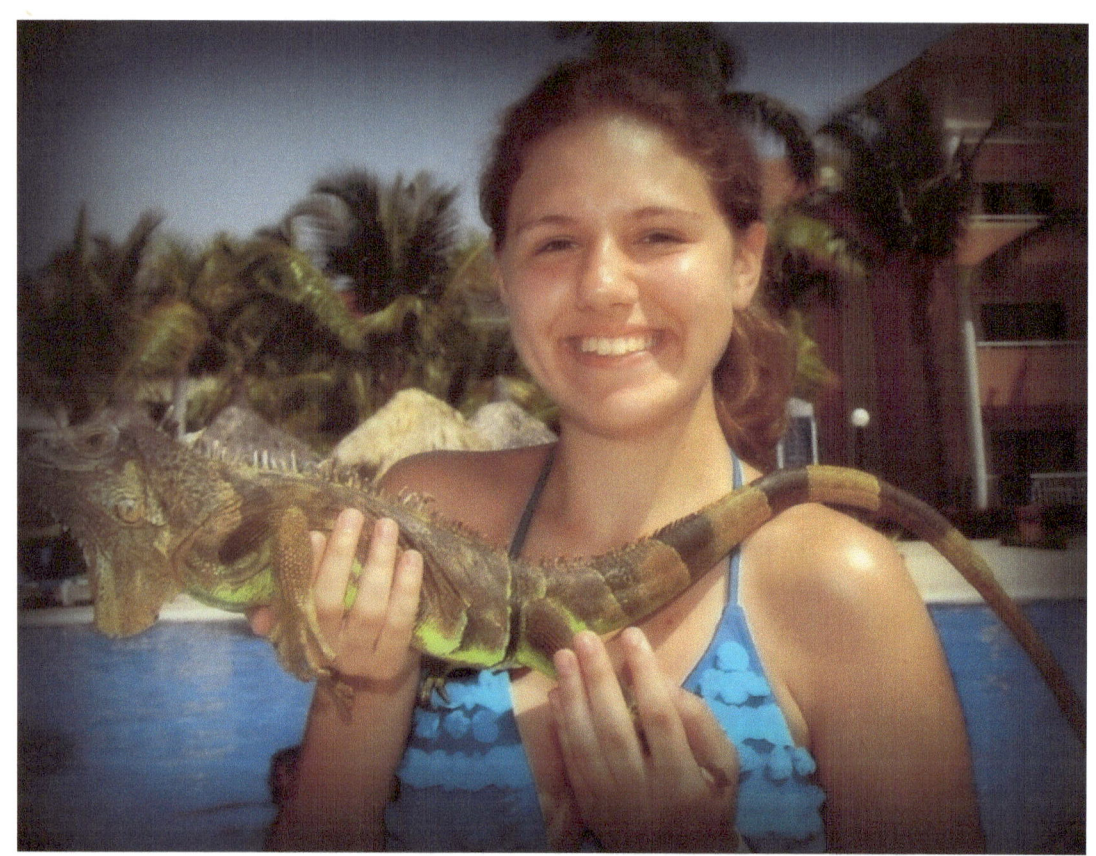

Lydia and Friend

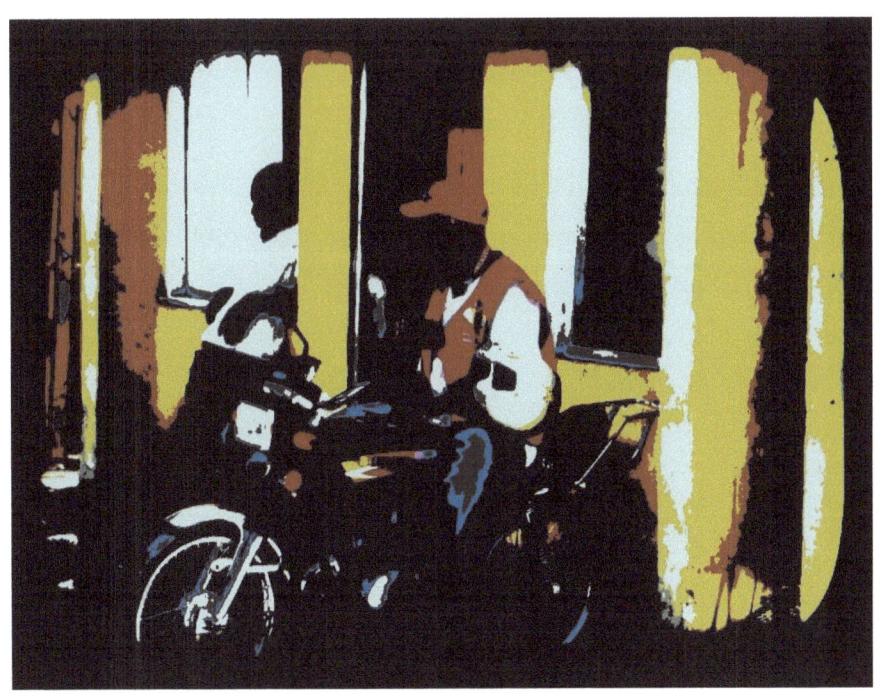

Biker Dudes

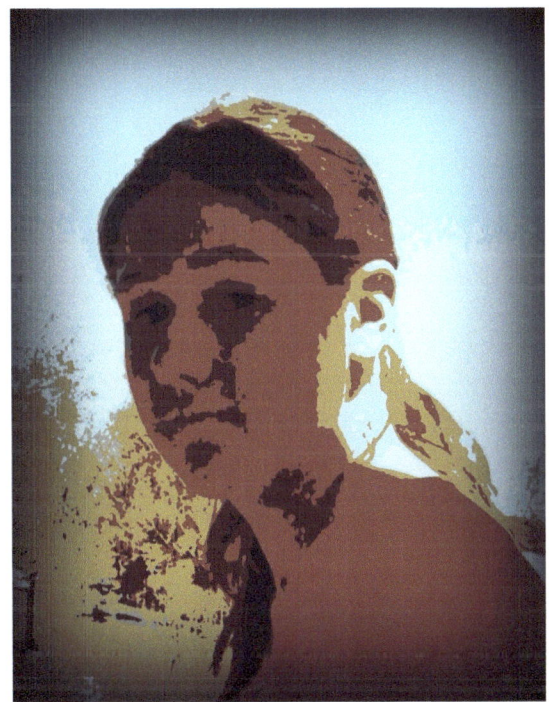

Lydia

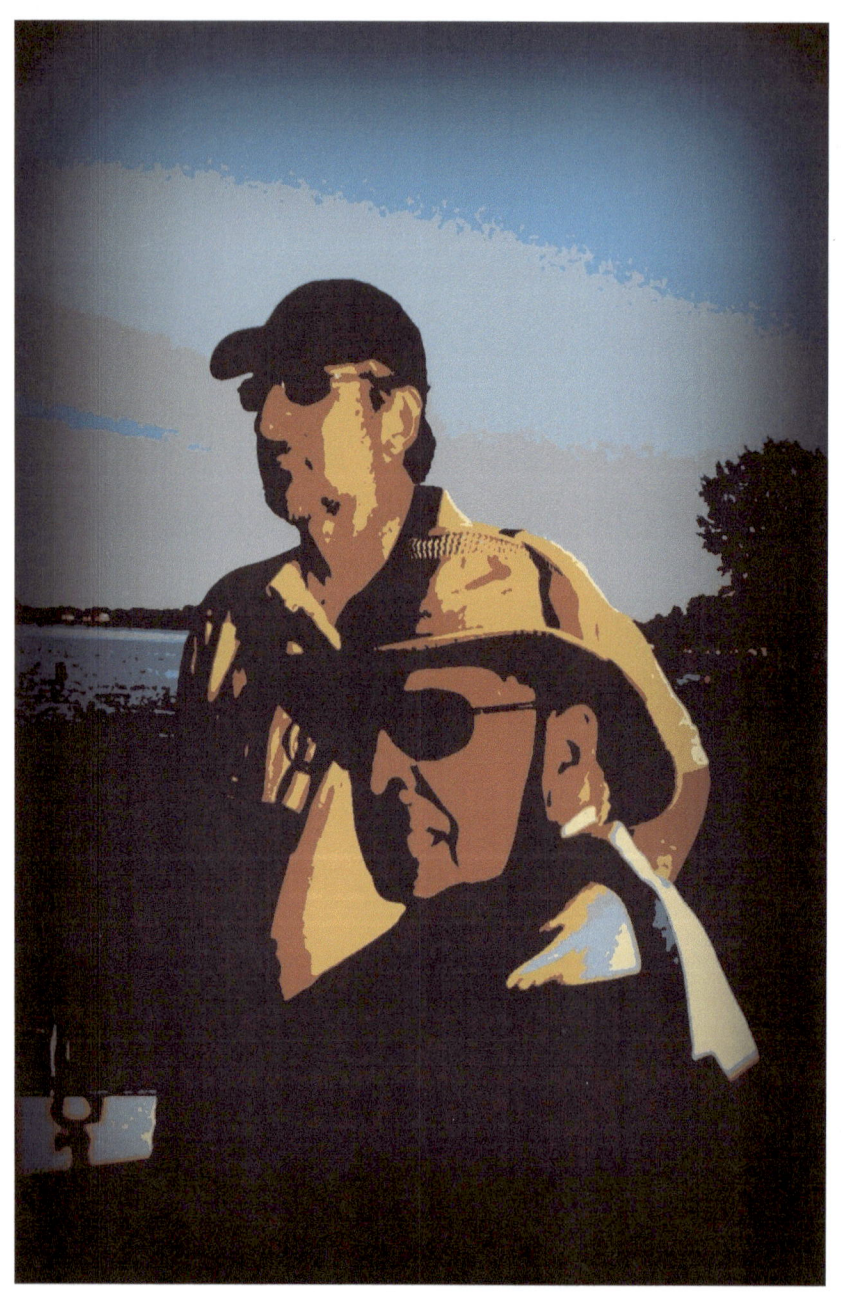

Friends of Ours

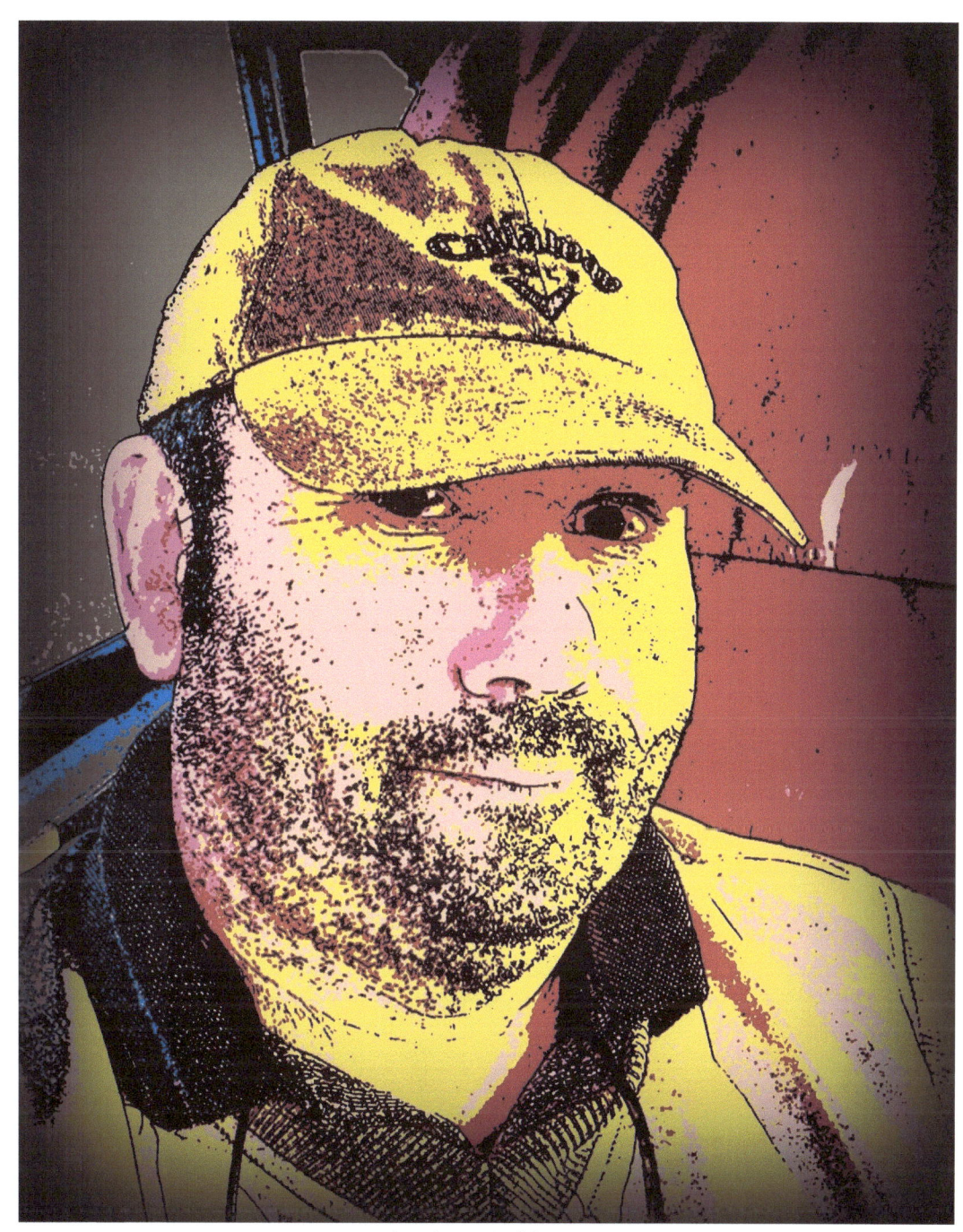

Ugly Fellow

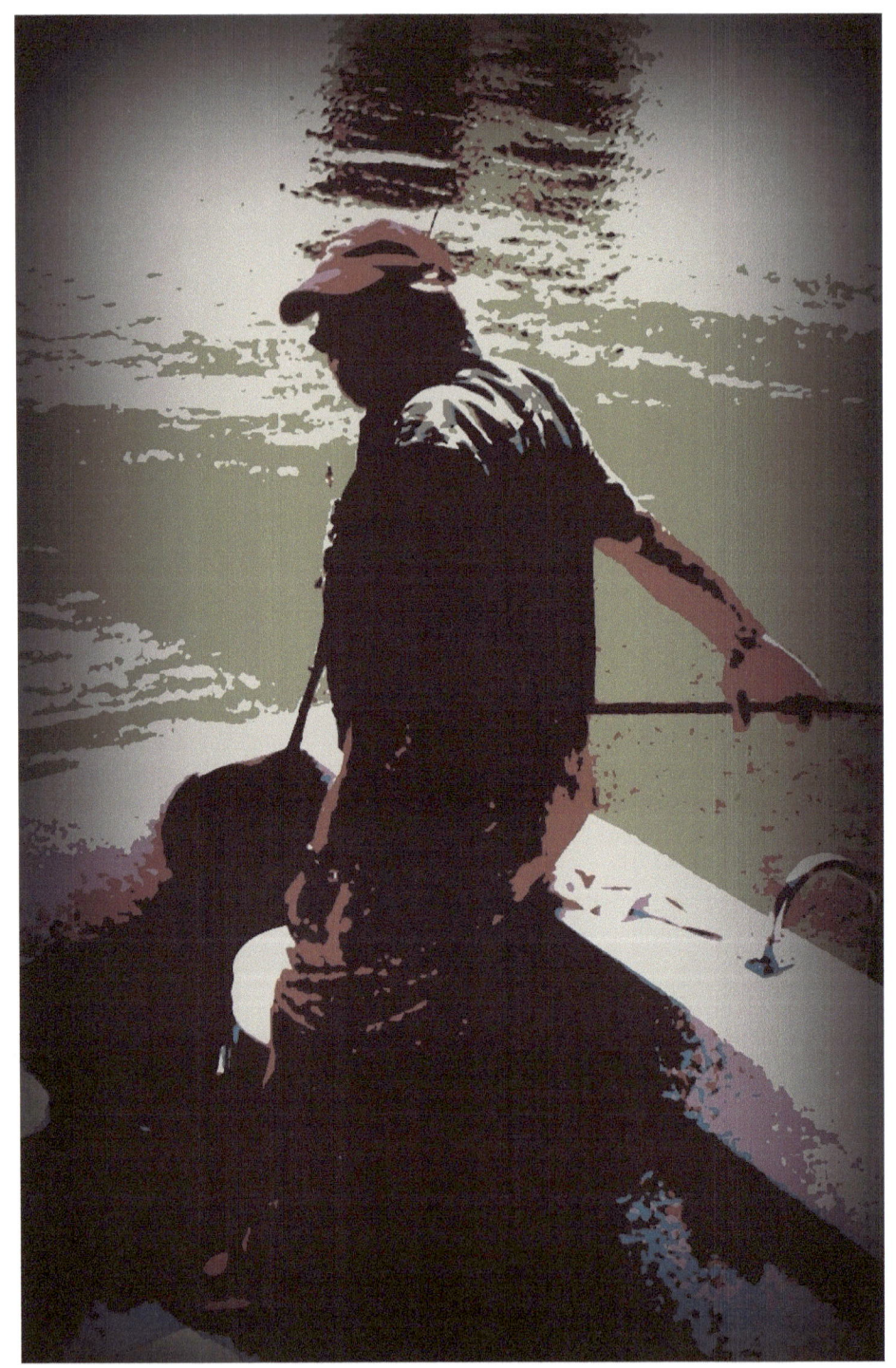

The Hock – Fishing

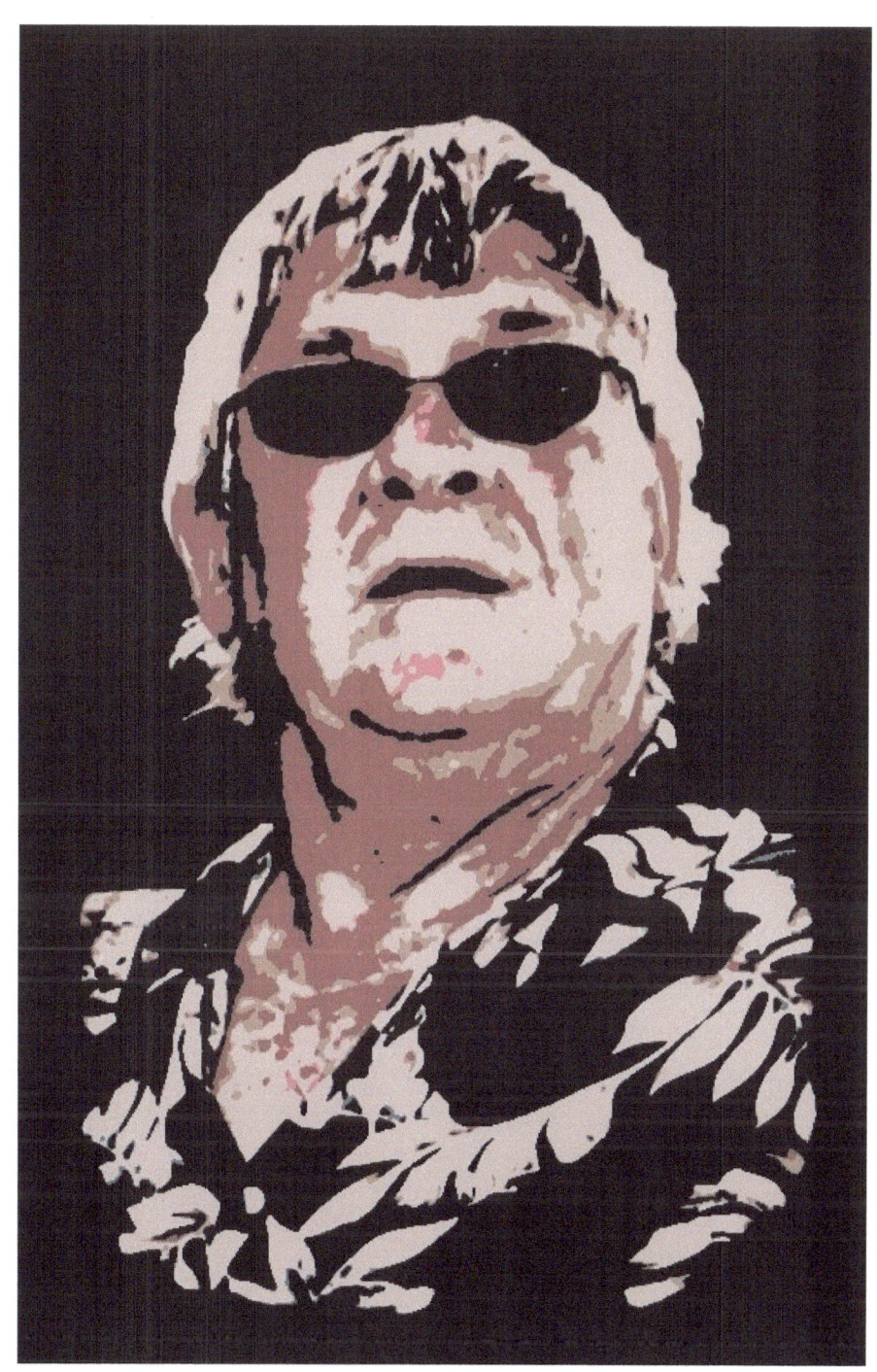

The Hock II

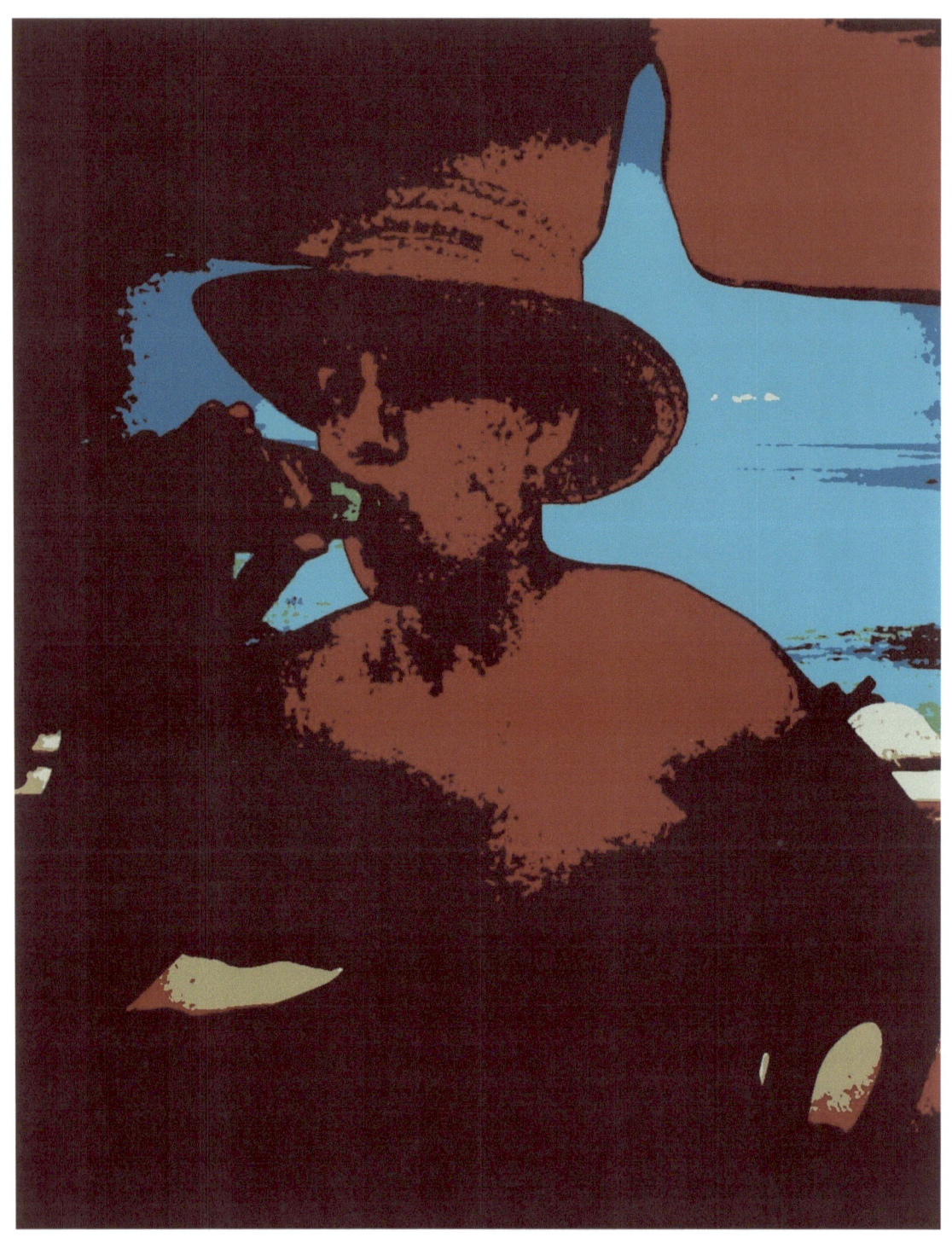

Jack in Jamaica

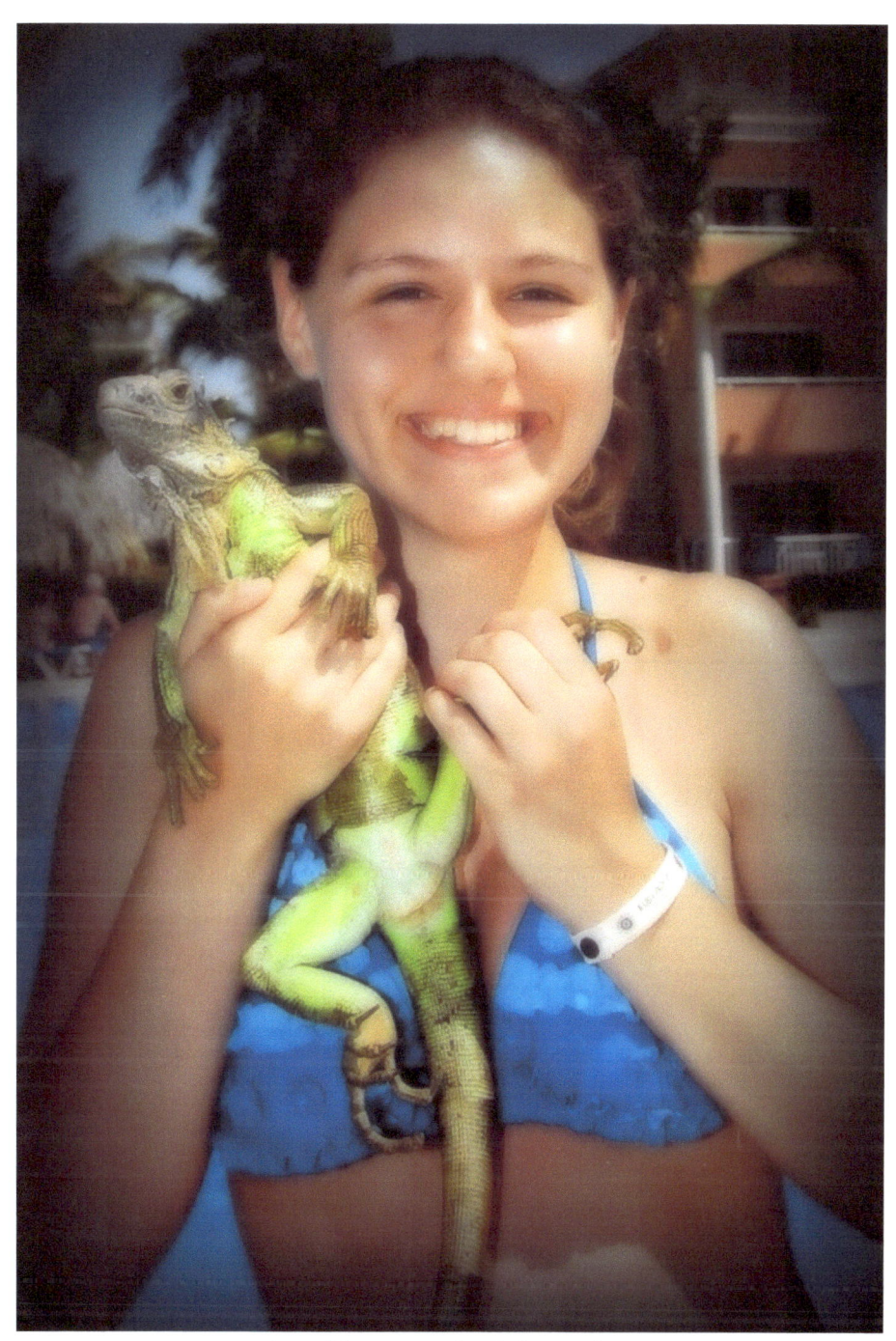

Lydia and Friend II

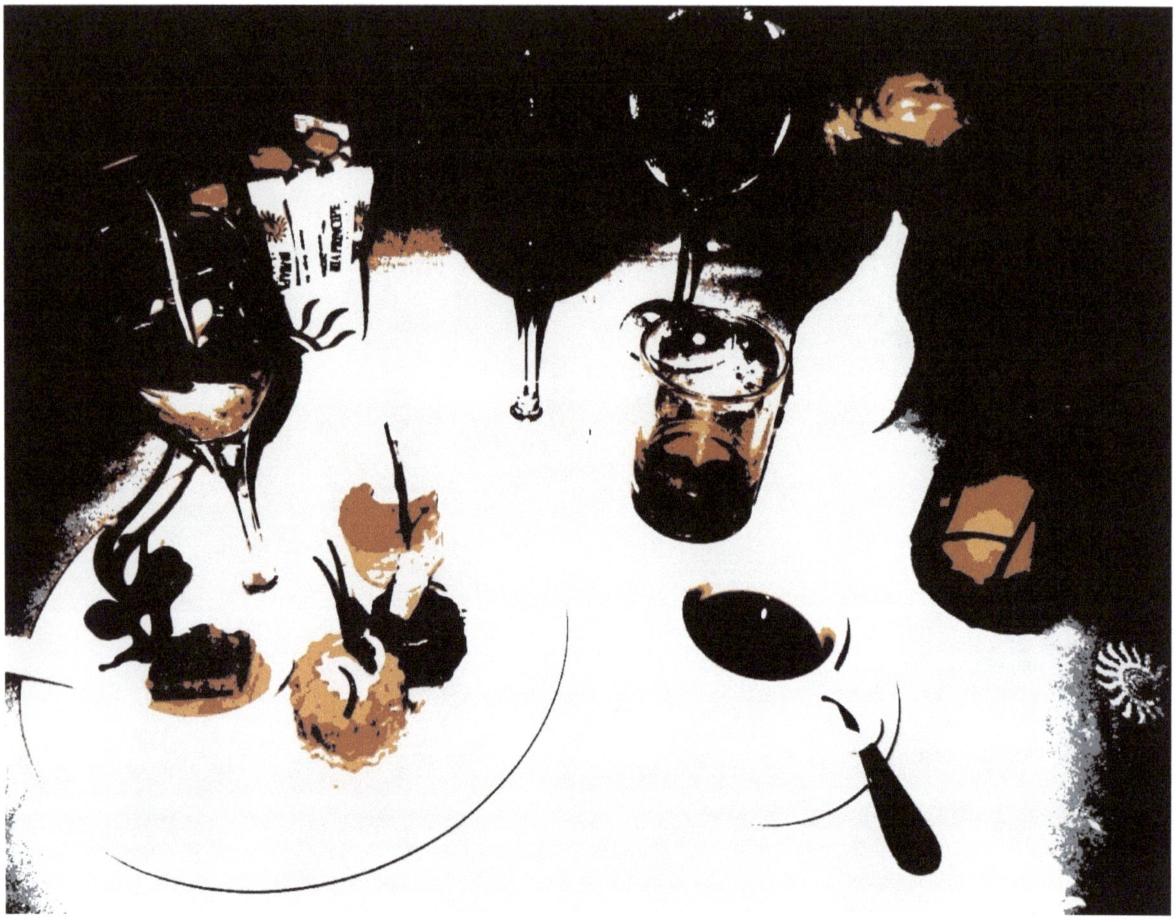

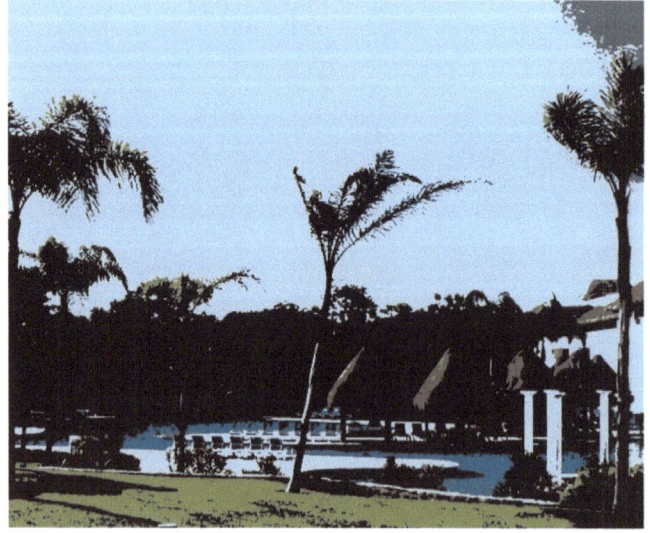

Sweet Time

By the Pool

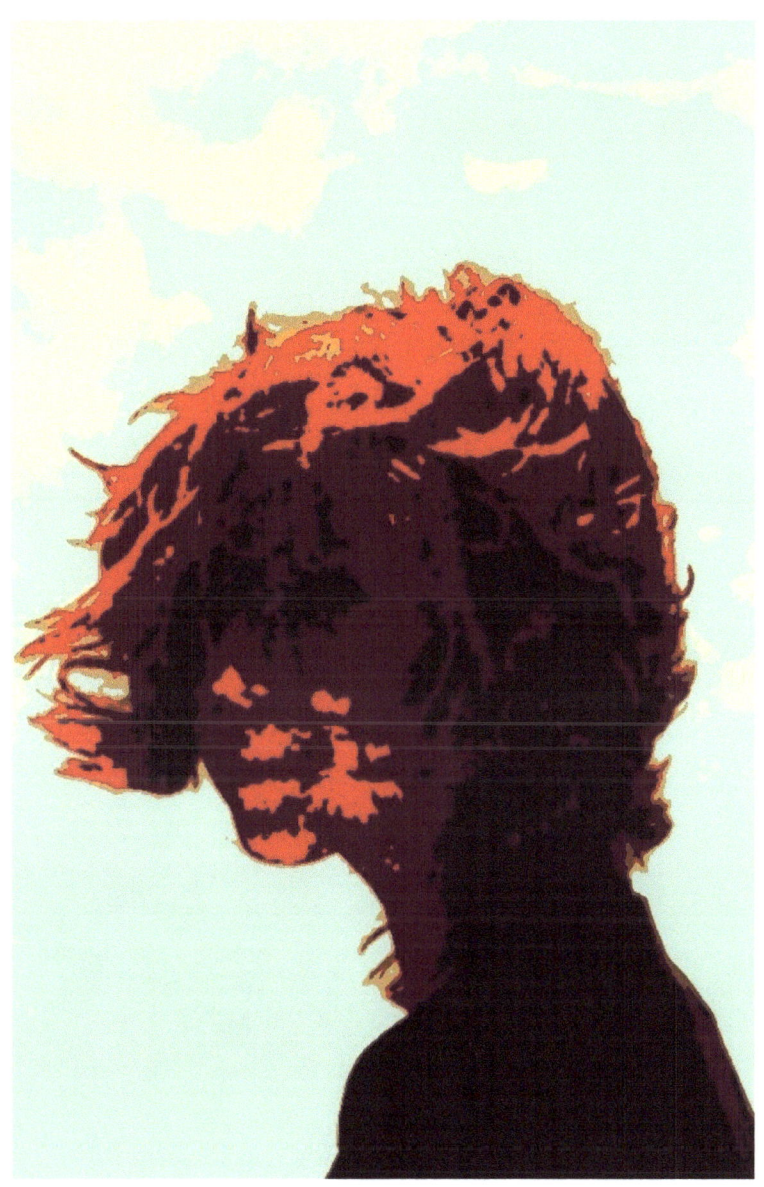

Alex

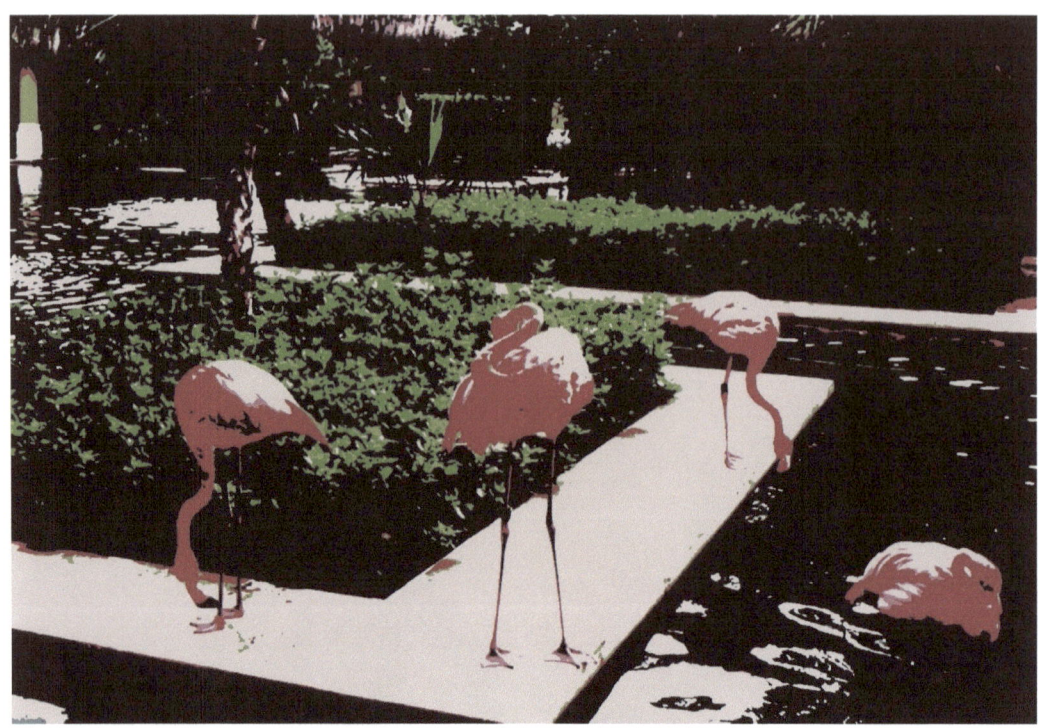

Birds of a Feather

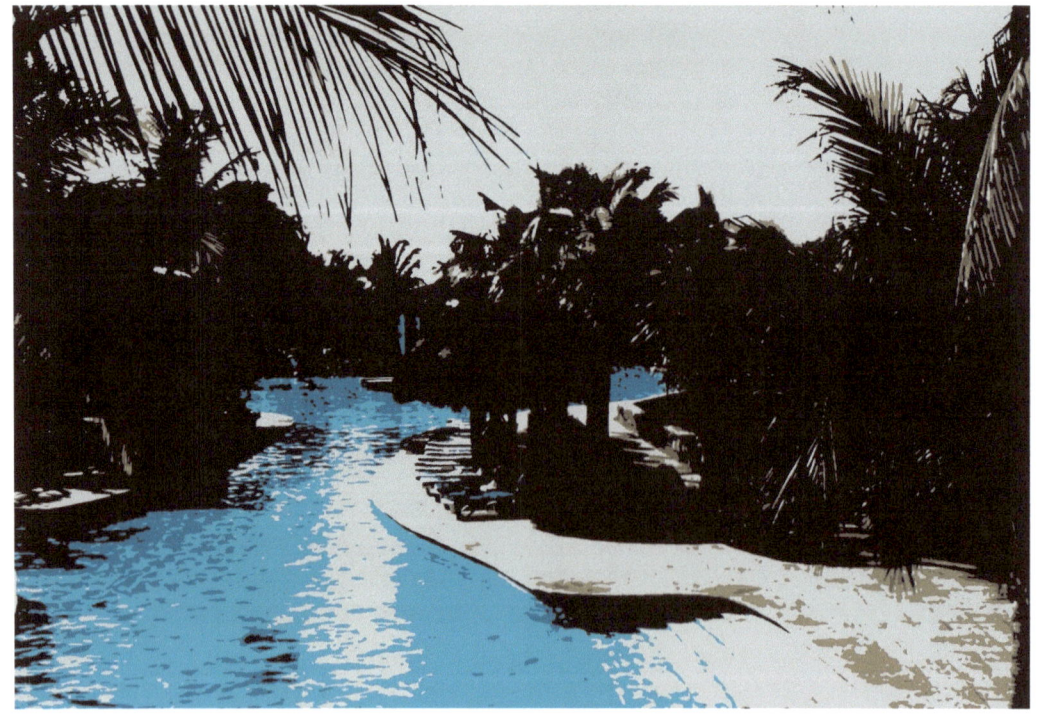

Poolside

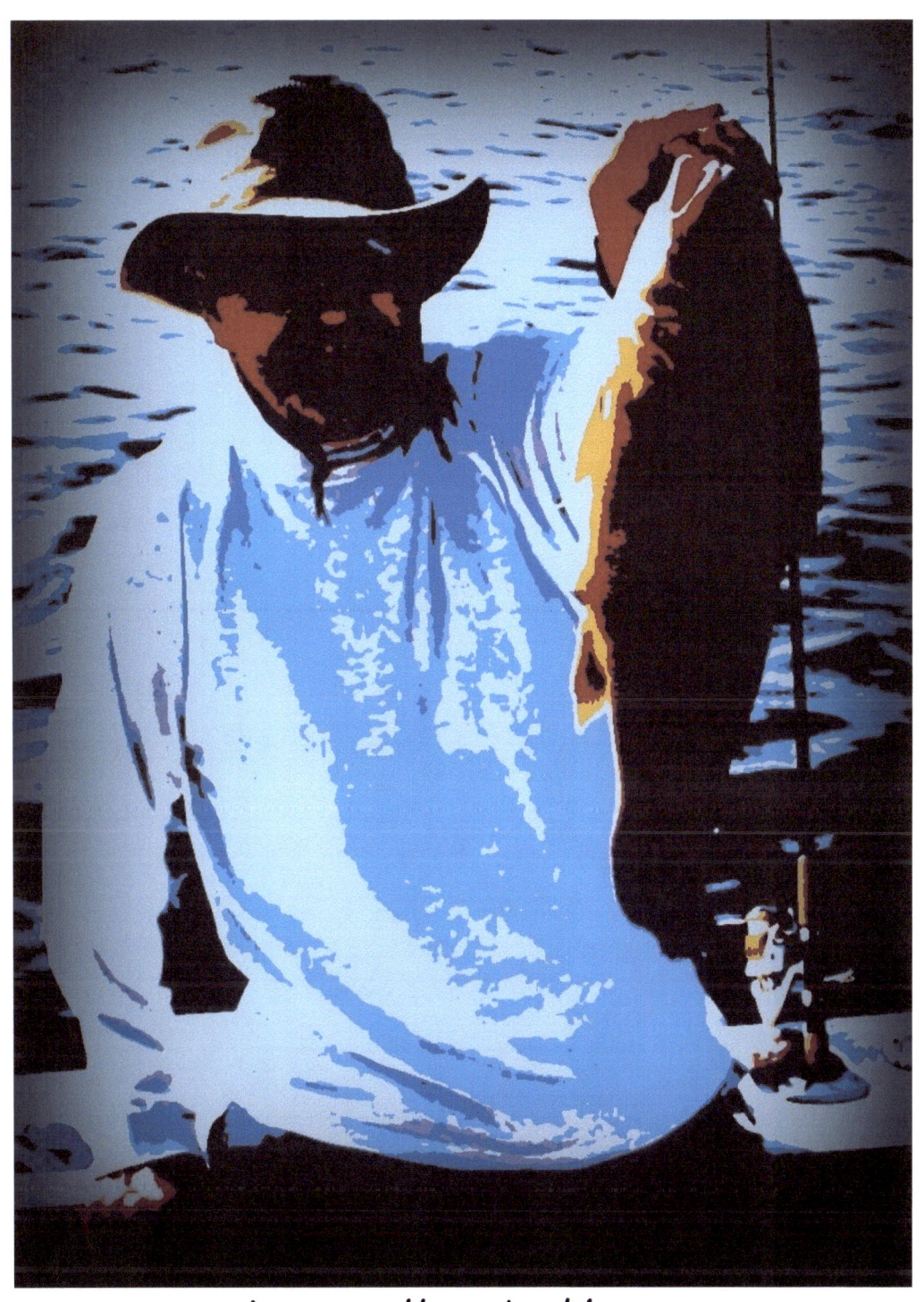

Larry pulls out a big one

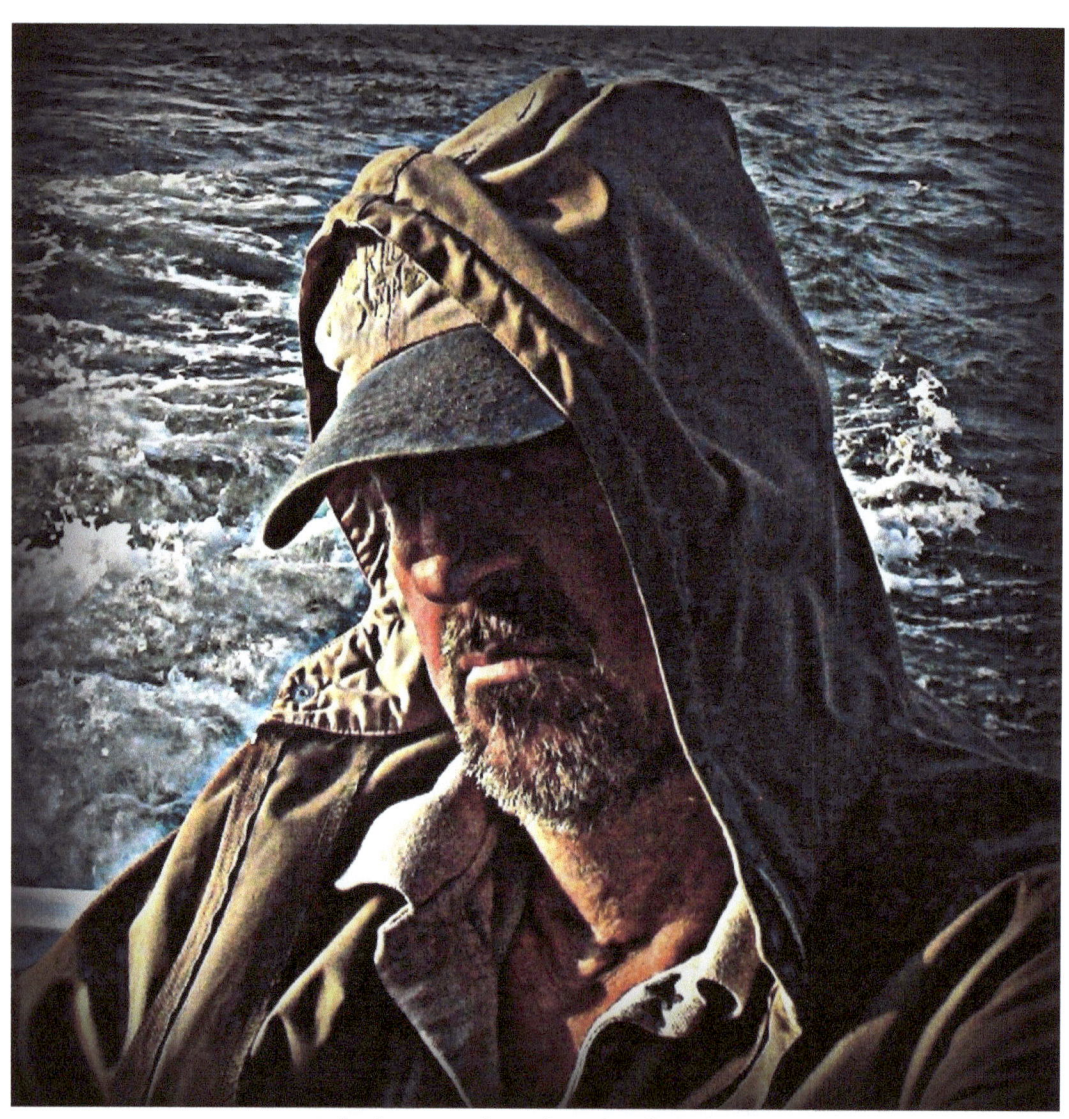

Rich – Tired of Fishing

www.ingramcontent.com/pod-product-compliance
Lightning Source LLC
Chambersburg PA
CBHW051023180526
45172CB00002B/446